DOCUMENTATION *and* INFORMATION RETRIEVAL

An Introduction to Basic Principles and Cost Analysis

BY J. W. PERRY
AND ALLEN KENT

Center for Documentation
and Communication Research
School of Library Science
Western Reserve University
Cleveland 6, Ohio

THE PRESS OF WESTERN RESERVE UNIVERSITY
AND INTERSCIENCE PUBLISHERS, INC.

FOREWORD

In the past we have repeatedly called attention to the danger that the techniques of librarianship -- its systems, its mechanisms, its corpus of practice -- may have out-distanced its fundamental theory. The techniques of the librarian have, for generations, been predicated upon implicit assumptions concerning man's utilization of recorded knowledge that often have not even been precisely enunciated, much less thoughtfully explored. The techniques of librarianship cannot, therefore, be subjected to indefinite refinement without eventually reaching stagnation, if not exhaustion. In a very real sense a technology is parasitic; it can thrive only so long as the fundamental theory upon which it feeds -- from which it derives its nourishment -- has vitality.

The poverty of innovation that now characterizes the profession of librarianship makes abundantly self-evident the need for a searching re-examination, based upon the findings of solid and dispassionate research, of the fundamental principles which underlie man's use of his recorded knowledge and the effects of that knowledge upon his behavior as an individual and as a social being. This is, indeed, a "very large order" and at the present time its ramifications can be but dimly perceived. Nevertheless, it is clear that the magnitude of such a study is sufficiently great that it cannot be accomplished by librarians working in isolation. They must draw upon many disciplines and enlist the assistance of specialists in a variety of fields; in mathematics, physics, chemistry, medicine, psychology, sociology, economics, and administration, to name but a few. Librarianship encompasses within its boundaries almost every aspect of man's need for and utilization of graphic records. The public library has, quite properly, regarded itself as a cohesive force in the community, a common ground on which men from every walk of life, with every form of intellectual interest, can meet in mutual understanding and equality of access to the written word. To its doors is

iii

brought the child for his first real contact with the world of books; to it comes the scholar seeking the most esoteric of treatises. Thus, as the library represents the synthesis of human experience, so librarianship itself must reaffirm the unity of knowledge and the interdependence of scholarship.

Librarians cannot, however, legitimately expect the specialists in other disciplines even to define the library problem, much less deliver it neatly solved on a silver platter. The librarian may look to his colleagues in other fields for knowledge which he himself does not and cannot have, but its application to the problem of improving recourse to graphic records must be accomplished by librarians.

Co-operation between librarian and subject specialist does not imply, one should emphasize, any sacrificial act on the part of either. The exchange should be mutually beneficial. This means more than improved access by the specialist to his own literature. The problems of librarianship can be a very fruitful area for exploration by many specialists, and this is particularly true in mathematics, logic, and other disciplines in which relationships are a primary consideration.

The study here presented has a dual purpose: (1) to promote an awareness of those aspects of the library problem which the mathematician and his associates in the physical sciences might fruitfully explore, even though they may never have regarded librarianship as a profitable object for their investigation, and (2) to give to librarians some indication of the ways in which certain of the precise sciences can be utilized in contributing to the solution of library problems, specifically in defining areas of fundamental research in librarianship and in planning experimental and mathematical models for research.

The present monograph is, however, a report of research in progress, and not a definitive statement of findings or results. To the thoughtful it will pose more questions than it answers, which is a characteristic of fundamental research. It initiates and, to a certain extent defines, one segment of the program of research which has been inaugurated at the School of Library Science at Western Reserve University. No one can yet foresee what the library world of fifty years hence will be, but there are indications that its technology may of necessity be

very different from that with which we are now familiar. It
is, therefore, particularly important that the fundamental
knowledge upon which that technology is to be erected and upon
which it will depend for its effectiveness must be equal to the
burden. We can no longer rely upon guess-work and subjective
opinion. We must analyze, we must measure, we must know.

Jesse H. Shera, Dean
School of Library Science

Western Reserve University
Cleveland, Ohio
March 30, 1951

PREFACE

During recent years, professional men in various fields have been confronted with increasingly difficult problems in making efficient use of recorded knowledge. In science and technology, for example, publication rates have maintained a record-breaking pace, particularly since the conclusion of World War II. The practical necessity of coping with information problems has resulted in much time and effort being devoted to development of new methods and techniques. Much of this development has been directed to some specific practical situation. At times, development efforts in this field have failed, to a surprising degree, to take account of basic underlying principles.

This monograph has been written in the conviction that mathematical formulation of basic principles together with cost analysis of procedures and operations will permit the development of information systems to be placed on a firm engineering basis. This goal can scarcely be achieved by a single book. It is hoped, however, that this book, by directing attention to basic principles may contribute to placing the development of information methods and systems on a firmer basis, especially with regard to the analysis of costs and the forecasting of capabilities and limitations.

The present monograph is accordingly directed to a basic theory of information retrieval and correlation. Experience has shown that these operations are of key importance in making effective use of recorded information, especially large files of graphic records. It seems reasonable to expect that an effective theory for information retrieval and correlation may provide the keystone for a general theory of documentation, which for present purposes might be defined as communication by means of graphic records.

The practical considerations that provide impetus to documentation research are not discussed in this monograph.

Rather the reader is referred to two books which summarize, in successive decades, the importance of documentation and documentation research to scientific research, in particular, and to professional activity, in general:

1. "Royal Society Scientific Information Conference," 12 June - 2 July 1948; report and papers submitted. London, The Royal Society, 1948.

2. "Documentation in Action," edited by J. H. Shera, A. Kent, and J. W. Perry. New York, Reinhold, 1956. (Proceedings of the Conference on the Practical Utilization of Recorded Knowledge, Western Reserve University, Cleveland, Ohio, January 16-18, 1956).

Increasing awareness of the practical importance of documentation research has stimulated the development of a considerable variety of devices, methods, and systems, particularly during the past decade. For recent summaries of these developments with particular attention to capabilities and limitations, the reader is referred to the following reviews and books:

1. "Inventory of Methods and Devices for Analysis, Storage and Retrieval of Information", by M. R. Hyslop and others, "Documentation in Action", op. cit, pp. 101-136.

2. "Punched Cards. Their Application to Science and Industry", edited by R. S. Casey and J. W. Perry. New York, Reinhold, 1951 (second edition in preparation).

3. "The Classified Catalog," by J. H. Shera and M. Egan. Chicago, A. L. A., 1956.

4. "Machine Literature Searching," by J. W. Perry, A. Kent, and M. M. Berry. New York, Interscience, 1956.

5. "Studies in Coordinate Indexing," by M. Taube and Associates. Washington, D. C., Documentation, Inc., Vols. 1-3, 1953-5.

6. "Two Methods of Organizing Technical Information for Search," L. M. Bohnert, American Documentation, 6, 134-151 (July 1955).

7. "Advances in Documentation and Library Science", Vol.I, edited by G. L. Peakes, A. Kent, and J. W. Perry. New York, Interscience, 1957 (in press).

The philosophy of documentation and retrieval of non-

numerical data as it differs from problems of retrieval of
numerical data will not be discussed in detail. Rather, the
reader is referred to two references, as follows:
1. "Classification and Indexing in Science", by B. C.
    Vickery, book in preparation.
2. "Requirements and Procedures in Documentation and
    Machine Literature Searching", J. W. Perry and Allen
    Kent, Journal of Documentation, manuscript submitted
    for publication.

ACKNOWLEDGEMENTS

The authors are indebted to Rome Air Development Center,
Department of the Air Force; to Development and Proof Services,
Aberdeen Proving Ground; to the American Society for Metals;
and many other sponsors for the support which made possible
the studies reported here.

CONTENTS

CHAPTER I

GENERAL STATEMENT

Communication by means of graphic records--especially communication across the time barrier--often leads to the accumulation of large numbers of records. Efficient use of the information they contain requires, in turn, the ability to identify those records of pertinent interest to a given problem or situation. Such selection is, fundamentally, a process of class definition, in which the characteristics of the subject contents of the documents are of decisive importance in effecting useful classification or grouping.

The problem of characterizing important aspects of recorded information for subsequent identification, correlation, and retrieval from large files has, historically, been approached from two points of view that are sometimes regarded as much more divergent in character than they actually are. These two approaches are the following:

(1) Arraying in a predetermined order or set of groups in advance of definition of specific information requirements. (Library classification of books or pigeonhole classification of patents may be cited as examples. The usefulness of this approach is determined by the extent to which a preestablished array can satisfy future information requirements).

(2) Identifying records of pertinent interest subsequent to definition of an information requirement. (Such identification is achieved on the basis of various characteristics, usually taken in combination, though individual characteristics may be effective in some circumstances).

The first approach is static in character as it is based on preestablished arrays. The essential equipment consists of devices, such as pigeonholes, that are effective in maintaining fixed arrays. The second approach requires a selection to be performed whenever an information request is serviced. The

1

equipment used must perform or, at least, facilitate such
selection and it is, consequently, quite different in nature.

In spite of differences in equipment and in operational
methods, both approaches are based on the analysis of subject
contents of documents as to characteristics. Differences between the two approaches may be regarded as different ways
of making use of the characteristics of documents to establish
useful groupings. As a consequence, a basis is provided for
development of a general theory of information retrieval and
correlation. The present monograph is devoted to the development of a general theory for both the more traditional procedures, especially alphabetized indexing and pigeon-hole
classification, as well as more recently developed systems
for accomplishing selection by automatic or semi-automatic
devices.

The practical importance of the theoretical analysis is
emphasized by directing attention to various cost factors
involved in actual operation and by discussion of their relative
magnitudes.

For presentation purposes, this monograph is organized
in five parts:

(1) A mathematical model which defines the basic opera-
     tions of characterizing and grouping and investigates
     their nature.
(2) An analysis of costs of storing recorded information
     in documents.
(3) An analysis of systems using grouping principles, e. g.,
     "pigeon-hole" classification, multi-aspect classifica-
     tion, whether operated manually or mechanically;
(4) An analysis of systems using characterizing prin-
     ciples, e. g., alphabetized indexes, "aspect" systems,
     whether operated manually or mechanically.
(5) A glossary of terms.

The mathematical discussion has been kept at an elementary level. Many persons in the library and documentation
profession are--almost traditionally--not mathematically
minded.

On the other hand, the mathematical discussion is intended to provide encouragement to engineers and scientists

who have concerned themselves with these problems--encour-
agement that the seemingly amorphous problems of dealing
with non-numerical, conceptual data are capable of exact
expression and thus amenable to mathematical analysis similar to that encountered in science and engineering.

CHAPTER II

A MATHEMATICAL MODEL SYSTEM

A. Introduction

This chapter directs attention to basic principles that underlie the development of various information retrieval systems. More specifically this chapter is concerned with those potentialities and capabilities of information retrieval systems that are related to the characterization of the subject contents of documents and to the use of characteristics--either singly or in combination--to effect identifying and selective operations. In dealing with large volumes of information, such operations must be performed as rapidly as possible and with minimum requirements of time and effort on the part of professional personnel. As a consequence, it is a matter of extreme practical importance to accomplish the processing of information by routines performed either clerically or by automatic equipment.

In actual situations, as encountered in practice, the formulation and definition of methods and procedures must take into account the purposes to be served and the circumstances under which a given system must be operated. In defining methods and procedures and in designing systems, it is, however, essential to take into account certain basic principles that underlie the analysis of the subject contents of documents and, in particular, the application of well-defined routines to identifying documents of pertinent interest to a given problem or situation.

These basic principles are explored and developed in this chapter. The relationship of these principles to various methods and procedures for information retrieval is pointed out with the aid of various examples. This review of basic principles and their application is believed essential to achieving optimum advantages when developing information retrieval systems to serve practical purposes.

A mathematical model is used as the means for defining and presenting basic principles.

In dealing with actual documents, careful attention must be directed to the scope of information requirements and to the nature of available information. More specifically, attention must be directed to the definition of concepts and terminology, to consistency in the use of concepts to analyze the subject contents of documents, and to the use of symbols (1) to represent and to record the results of the analysis both of subject content of documents and also of information requirements and (2) to plan and to control the performance of routine operations.

Viewed from the point of view of routine operations, decisive importance attaches to the basic operations of (1) characterizing the subject contents of documents in terms of well-defined concepts, and (2) conducting searching, selecting and grouping operations defined in terms of such concepts. To focus attention on these operations, it is highly desirable that problems of a semantic nature relating to the definition of concepts be relegated temporarily to the background. In this way it becomes possible to investigate the nature of the basic operations of (1) characterizing objects in terms of concepts and (2) using such concepts to effect selection and grouping to meet practical needs. An investigation along these lines thus provides the basis (1) for defining operations to be conducted routinely and (2) for resolving questions as to the definition of concepts and their consistent application in analyzing the subject contents of documents and the scope of information requirements.

Accordingly, in order that attention may be focused on the basic operations of characterizing and grouping, a mathematical model is presented. Investigation of this model leads to the formulation of principles for planning such basic operations as (1) close study of factual data or of abstract concepts in order to achieve the consistent characterization of each, and (2) the selection and grouping of various items in terms of individual characteristics or combinations of characteristics. This preliminary step provides a basis (1) for the analysis of the subject contents of documents with the aid of well-defined

characteristics and categories of characteristics and (2) for
conducting searching and correlating operations defined in
terms of such characteristics and combinations of characteristics. To illustrate such application of the mathematical
model, reference is made, by way of example, to alphabetized
indexing, compartmentalized classification, and certain more
general forms of analyzing and coding the subject contents of
documents.

B. Description of the Model

The model system to be described and analyzed has been
selected so as to provide (1) a finite number of objects to be
indexed, classified or otherwise analyzed, for selection and
grouping, (2) a small number of criteria that characterize the
objects under consideration and (3) the possibility of organizing these criteria into a small number of independent sets.

The objects with which this model system is concerned
may be visualized as similar to the building blocks that sometimes serve as childrens' toys. Each object will be characterized in ten different ways as follows: shape, size, material
of construction, surface texture or finish, color, presence of
a designation consisting of an Arabic or Roman numeral and
also an upper case and lower case letter as well as one of ten
special symbols. Each of these ten modes of characterization
corresponds to a set of criteria as presented in Figure 1. (Page 8)
Thus, one set of criteria refers to shape, namely, cube, other
parallelopiped, tetrahedron, etc. Another set of criteria refers to color, namely, red, yellow, green, etc. and various
shades of color.

We may summarize Figure 1 by the statement that we are
dealing with ten sets of characteristics with the various separate sets made up of specific characteristics as follows:

Set Number	Number and Type of Characteristics in Various Sets
1	10 shapes
2	100 materials
3	100 colors and shades of color
4	10 surface textures
5	100 values of largest transverse diameter

Set Number	Number and Type of Characteristics in Various Sets
6	10 Arabic numerals
7	10 Roman numerals
8	26 lower case letters
9	26 upper case letters
10	10 special markings

If each object in our collection is characterized by one characteristic from each of the ten sets and if, furthermore, our collection contains an object for each of such combinations of characteristics, then we would have

$$10 \times 100 \times 100 \times 10 \times 100 \times 10 \times 10 \times 26 \times 26 \times 10$$

or 6.76×10^{13} objects in our collection.

C. The Model and Classification Systems

It is, perhaps, immediately obvious that the objects in our collection might be classified into groups in the same way as documents may be grouped into fixed arrays, e. g., pigeonhole classification of patents.

It is instructive to consider the various ways in which such classification systems might be set up. Thus, we might select any one of the 10 sets of characteristics for the initial subdivision. For example, we might select either shape, or material, or color and shades of color. Having made this first selection for the main subdivision, any one of the nine remaining sets of characteristics might be chosen in setting up the second subdivision. Thus, for example, we might have, as main and later subdivisions in different classification systems, such combinations as the following:

Classification system 1
1. Shape
  2. Material
    3. Color
      4. Surface texture
        5. Largest transverse dimension
          6. Arabic numeral
             etc.
Classification system 2
1. Shape
  2. Color

Figure 1

Sets of Criteria for Characterizing Objects
for a Mathematical Model of Document Analysis

1. Shape - 10 characteristics (cube, other parallelopiped,
    sphere, tetrahedron, pyramid, truncated pyramid, cone,
    truncated cone, cylinder, ellipsoid).

2. Material - 10 general characteristics (with 10 specific
    characteristics under each)
    Pure metal (Ti, Zn, Cu, Au, Ag, Al, Fe, V, Zr, Cr),
    ferrous alloy (1-10), non-ferrous alloy (1-10), plastic
    derived from cellulose (1-10), other plastic (1-10), glass
    (1-10), other ceramic (1-10), wood (1-10), edible mater-
    ial (1-10), other material (1-10)

3. Color - 10 general characteristics (with 10 specific
    characteristics under each)
    Red (10 shades of red), yellow, green, blue, orange,
    purple, gray, brown, pink, gray (10 shades of each)

4. Surface texture - 10 characteristics
    (Painted, rough, smooth, polished, various forms of
    surface protuberance or indentation)

5. Largest transverse dimension
    10 ranges with 10 specific values for each

6. Arabic numeral 0 - 9 (total of 10 characteristics)

7. Roman numeral I - X (total of 10 characteristics)

8. Lower case letter a - z (total of 26 characteristics)

9. Upper case letter A - Z (total of 26 characteristics)

10. Special marking - 10 characteristics, &, $, ¢, Σ, @,
    #, /, ;, ?, !.

        3. Material
          4. Arabic numeral
            5. Surface texture
               etc.

Classification system 3
    1. Material
      2. Color
        3. Shape
          4. Surface texture
             etc.

Etc.

Each such classification system would be built up of a set of main classes with each main class broken down into a set of subclasses and the latter subdivided in turn into further sub-subclasses and so on as indicated by "etc." in the examples above. Thus the first classification system would have as its main classes the ten shapes as listed in Figure 1. Under each shape there would be 100 subclasses corresponding to the hundred categories of materials and these in turn would be broken down into sub-subclasses corresponding to the various set of characteristics we may have chosen in developing this particular classification system. We will return to further consideration of the classes and subclasses in such a classification system after first investigating the number of such classification systems that may be set up.

As noted above, any one of our ten sets of characteristics may be chosen to establish the main classes in a classification system. Once this choice has been made, any one of the remaining nine sets of characteristics may be chosen for the first subdivision under the main classes, for the next subdivision any one of the eight remaining sets may be chosen and so on. Thus the number of distinct classification systems that may be set up based on 10 sets of characteristics may be determined by multiplying:

$$10 \times 9 \times 8 \times 7 \times 6 \times 5 \times 4 \times 3 \times 2 \times 1$$

a product which mathematicians denote as 10!.

In general, if L is the number of sets of characteristics, then the number, U_c, of classification systems that may be set up as indicated above will be given by the equation

$$U_c = L!$$

Obviously L! increases very rapidly as L becomes larger.
The following examples illustrate this point:

L	U_c	L	U_c
1	1	6	720
2	2	7	5,040
3	6	8	40,320
4	24	9	362,880
5	120	10	3,628,800

For convenience in illustrating the structure of such
classification systems, U_c, in number and built up of L sets
of characteristics, we will refer, by way of example, during
our discussion to a simple case in which the number of sets
of characteristics is 10 and the number of characteristics in
each set is also 10. (In our more general mathematical model
most of the sets of characteristics contained 10 characteristics per set, but a few of the sets contained 100 characteristics and a few of the sets contained 26 characteristics per set.)
For the simplified case under consideration, Figure 2 shows
ten main classes (L = 10). A lesser number of sets than L
may be used to establish a classification. This lesser number
we will denote by j. Figure 2 shows the subdivision of classes
into subclasses and sub-subclasses with j increasing from
1 to 10. The subdivision of each main class into subclasses
is shown for main class 4 only, because of lack of space in the
diagram. Similarly in Figure 2, only one set of ten subdivisions is shown at each level. Actually, the number of such
subdivisions would increase very rapidly as j becomes larger.
For example, if j had been 3, we would have 10 x 10 x 10 or
1,000 subsubclasses, each of which would be broken down in
10 further subdivisions if j is increased to 4.

In the simple case under consideration, decimal notation
may be used to designate the various classes, subclasses,
subsubclasses, etc. The number of digits used for designation
of a given subdivision will depend on the value of j. Thus if
three sets of characteristics are utilized for constructing a
classification system as shown in Figure 2, then j = 3 and the
most extensively subdivided subclasses would be denoted by
three digits, e.g., 456. In Figure 2, designation of class and
subclass is in terms of such digits followed by as many dashes

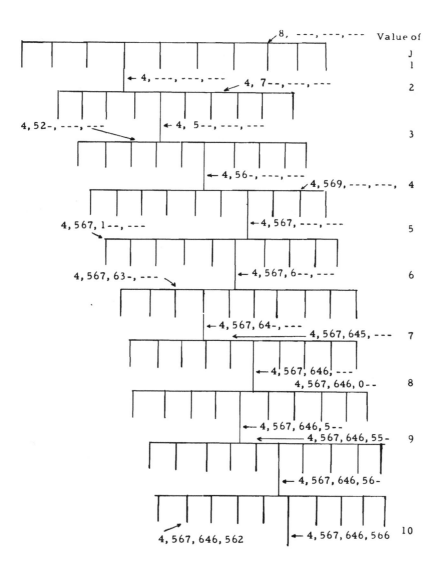

Figure 2.

Diagram to Illustrate Successive Subdivision of
Main Classes into Subclasses, Subsubclasses, etc.

as correspond to sets of characteristics not taken into account up to the level of subdivision under consideration. In Figure 2, decimal notation for one subdivision at each level has been provided and the further breakdown of that subdivision has been diagrammed. In addition, at each level, the decimal notation has been provided for an additional subdivision whose further breakdown is not diagrammed.

In the simple case shown in Figure 2, the number of subdivisions at any level is determined by the value of j. Thus, if we set up a classification system with three sets of characteristics (j = 3), the number of smallest subdivisions established would be 10^3 or 1,000. Here, ten characteristics compose each set of the same. In the more general case, the number of characteristics per set will vary. Thus, the general case might be illustrated as follows:

Level, j   1, 2, 3, 4, 5, --- j ----- L

General symbol for num-
    ber of characteristics in
    a set at a given level u_1, u_2, u_3, u_4, u_5 -- u_j ----- u_L

Specific example of num-
    ber of characteristics   5, 14, 27, 8, 5 --- 10 ----- 20

Here, as before, the number of subdivisions in the classification system, increases as we pass to larger values of j and the number of such subdivisions for the general case may be given as follows:

Level of Subdivision (j)	Number of Characteristics per Set in the Specific Case (u)	Number of Subdivisions in the Specific Case (M)
1	u_1 = 5	5
2	u_2 = 14	90
3	u_3 = 27	1430
4	u_4 = 8	11440
5	u_5 = 5	57200

The general formula for the number of subdivisions at the j-th level in such a classification system would be:

$$M_j = \Pi u_j$$

where the symbol Π indicates multiplication to arrive at the product of all the u_j terms from $j = 1$ to $j = j$. This formula, it should be emphasized, gives the number of subdivisions at any one level in any one classification system.

(1) Derived Characteristics from Model

If we now direct attention to the mathematical model defined by Figure 2 and the accompanying description, it may be observed that establishment of classification systems may be accomplished by basing subdivision not on the individual characteristics as listed, but on a less discriminating characterization. Thus, we might decide, with regard to shape, not to distinguish between spheres and cubes or between cones and pyramids or between truncated pyramids and truncated cones or between cylinders and ellipsoids. Such a decision would then reduce to six the number of shape characteristics, which would then become the following:

Characteristic Number	Characteristic
i	Cube and/or sphere
ii	Pyramid and/or cone
iii	Truncated pyramid and/or truncated cone
iv	Cylinder and/or ellipsoid
v	Other parallelopiped
vi	Tetrahedron

Thus all objects that are either cubes or spheres would be within the scope of our above noted derived characteristic i, all objects that are either pyramids or cones within the scope of characteristic ii, etc. These examples illustrate one way in which basic characteristics may be combined to generate additional characteristics which we will speak of as "derived characteristics". More specifically these examples illustrate how basic characteristics may be combined on an "and/or" basis to generate derived characteristics. Such "and/or" combinations we shall refer to as derived characteristics based on logical sums. In the general case, a logical sum of basic characteristics is not limited to two characteristics as in the

example just cited.   For example we might generate a derived
characteristic as the logical sum of:

cube and/or sphere and/or pyramid and/or cone

(A)   (B)   (C)   (D)

which we might symbolize as:

A + B + C + D

Another way in which derived characteristics may be generated is to base their definition on the simultaneous presence
of two or more characteristics, each from a different set.
Thus we might define as a derived characteristic, the combination of properties:

"spherical shape, made of gold, painted red"

Since this method of generating derived characteristics requires that each of two or more basic characteristics shall be
present, we may, in general, denote such derived characteristics by a logical product, which may be represented,

A · B · C

This procedure makes it possible to define very large numbers
of derived characteristics in terms of combinations of a small
or limited number of basic characteristics and formulas will
be presented subsequently for calculating the number of derived characteristics that may be defined in terms of a given
number of basic characteristics.   For the moment, we will
limit discussion of this type of derived characteristic to noting
that the general method for their generation is closely related
to the generation of classes and subclasses on the basis of
combinations of basic characteristics as illustrated in Figure 2.

It is perhaps obvious that we may also generate derived
characteristics in terms of the presence of some characteristic
but the absence of another.   This type of derived characteristic
might be exemplified by

"sphere but not gold".

(A)   (B)

The presence of one characteristic and the absence of another
corresponds to a logical difference and may be symbolized by
A - B.   Thus the symbol A might refer to the characteristic
"sphere" and B might refer to "gold".

Derived characteristics may also be defined in terms of
more complex combinations of basic characteristics.   Thus

we might have the derived characteristic

"sphere or cube made of gold without the Roman numeral IV".
  (A)   (B)   (C)   (D)

Such a definition may be represented symbolically by

$$(A + B) (C - D)$$

where A denotes sphere
     B denotes cube
     C denotes gold
     D denotes Roman numeral IV.

Obviously, a very large number of derived characteristics may be generated in this way by establishing combinations of a relatively small number of basic characteristics. This is a point to which we shall return in subsequent discussion of terminology and its role in the analysis and correlation of recorded information.

(2) Defining and Establishing Subdivisions

The possibility of generating derived characteristics greatly extends the possibilities of defining and establishing subdivisions when constructing classification systems and establishing useful groupings in general. These possibilities are, as may be obvious, of great practical importance and they will require our subsequent attention. To provide a basis for considering the wide range of possibilities that arise from generation of derived characteristics, we must again direct attention to our mathematical model and in particular to the type of classification system exemplified by Figure 2. It will be recalled that this type of classification system is based on sets of basic characteristics and that each of the subdivisions within the classification system is characterized by a com-bination of basic characteristics so established that no more than one characteristic from any one set of characteristics may enter into the combination.

It will be recalled that we showed that the number of sub-divisions at the j - th level of such a classification system is given by the formula:

$$M_j = \Pi u_j$$

Before considering additional formulas of a general na-ture, it should be noted that the number of smallest subdivi-

based on the combination of all of L sets of characteristics is
given by:

$$M_L = u_1 \cdot u_2 \cdot u_3 \cdot u_4 --- u_L = \Pi u_L$$

This number is, of course, the number of different combinations of characteristics when such combinations are generated
by taking one characteristic (but no more than one) from each
set. Formation of combinations in this fashion is encountered
in practice when we are dealing with sets of mutually exclusive
characteristics. (Here, the term "mutually exclusive" indicates that use of a characteristic from a given set to generate
a combination excludes the possibility of other characteristics
from the same set entering the combination in question.) For
objects whose characteristics are mutually exclusive, the
total number of different objects is equal to the number of   .
smallest subdivisions in a classification system of the above
specified type. In other words, the various combinations of
all of L sets of characteristics define both the classification
subdivisions and the objects with ultimate subdivision result-
ing in definition of a subclass to correspond to each object in
the collection.

It will be recalled that with 10 sets of characteristics it
would be possible to construct 10! or 3,628,800 different
classification systems of the type under consideration. These
classification systems differ with respect to the hierarchial
sequence of the sets of characteristics in defining successive
levels of subdivision. More generally, with L sets of characteristics the number of such different classification systems
would be L!. Though these classification systems are all
different, their ultimate subdivisions would in all cases contain only a single object. Hence, at this level at least, the
content of the subdivision and subdivisions themselves would
be the same for all of our systems. The lowest level
subdivisions would differ, however, in the order in which the
various sets of characteristics are taken into account in proceeding from the initial main classes (j = 1) through subclasses, subsubclasses, etc., to the final subdivisions at the
ultimate (i.e. the L'th) level. Hence these final subdivisions
would differ from each other with regard to their mode of
definition but not with regard to their contents, namely, some
one object in each ultimate subdivision.

Similarly, with lower values of j, the objects that would be within the range of a given subdivision of one classification system may be the same as within some one subdivision of a differently constructed classification system. Thus, in terms of our model, we might have a classification system whose main classes are based on shape (sphere, cube, etc.) and the immediately following subclasses (j = 2) on material (pure metal, ferrous alloy, etc.) and also another classification system whose main classes are based on material and the immediately following (j = 2) subclasses on shape. A little reflection will reveal that in these two systems their subclasses (j = 2) may be paired off so that a given pair will be defined by the same combination of characteristics and such pairs of subclasses will embrace, obviously, the same group of objects. Such subclasses which differ with regard to the definition process but which embrace the same group of objects will be referred to as isometric or isometrically identical. When two subdivisions (e.g. main classes, subsubclasses, etc.) differ as to the objects that they embrace they will be termed isometrically distinct.

It is a matter both of theoretical and practical importance to take note of the number of isometrically distinct classes, subclasses and similar subdivisions that may be encountered in the totality of the L! classification systems of the type under consideration. In general, the various isometrically distinctive subdivisions can be defined by a number of different procedures. In other words, the L! classification systems may be regarded as consisting of subdivisions that may be grouped into sets of isometrically identical subdivisions. With a given set of such subdivisions, all of them would embrace the same group of objects but each of the subdivisions within such a set would differ from its companions by a different procedure of definition. It should be emphasized that no one of our L! classification systems will contribute more than one subdivision to any given set of isometrically identical subdivisions. In fact, no one of our classification systems will contribute a subdivision to each of the totality of isometrically identical sets. This is a most important practical point as it is equivalent to saying that no one of the L! classification systems achieves all possible groupings of the objects that constitute our model system.

To establish the formula for the number of isometrically distinct sets of subdivisions, let us consider, as before, a set of objects with L sets of characteristics with the number of characteristics in different sets being denoted by u_1, u_2, u_3, u_4 --- u_j --- u_L. Then at the j - th level of the L! classification systems, the total number of possible different ways in which the sets of characteristics may be combined is given by the formula for L things taken j at a time. Thus C_{s_j} the number of combinations of L sets of characteristics taken j at a time will be:

$$C_{s_j} = \frac{L!}{j! \, (L - j)!}$$

Each of these combinations will, obviously, consist of j sets of characteristics. For any one combination, each of its component j sets of characteristics will consist of a number of characteristics which, for successive sets, we will denote by u_i, u_{ii}, u_{iii}, u_{iv} --- u_j. The number, N_{s_j} of isometrically distinct sets of subdivisions at the j level will then be given, in line with previous reasoning by:

$$N_{s_j} = u_i \cdot u_{ii} \cdot u_{iii} \cdot u_{iv} \text{ --- } u_j = \Pi u_j$$

The totality number, N_s, of isometrically distinct sets of subdivisions at all levels in our classification systems would be the sum of distinct sets at each level, or:

$$N_s = N_{s_1} + N_{s_2} + N_{s_3} + N_{s_4} \text{ --- } + N_{s_j} \text{ --- } + N_{s_L}$$

Within one of the isometrically distinct sets, its component subdivisions may be distinguished by mode of definition. As already noted, such differences in mode of definition arise when the same combinations of sets of characteristics is built up by a different hierarchial order of sets of characteristics in different classification systems. At the j - th level, each of the N_{s_j} isometrically distinctive sets involves, obviously, j sets of characteristics. The number of different hierarchial orders of combination of j sets of characteristics is equal to j!, i.e., the product

$$j \ (j - 1) \ (j - 2) \ \text{---} \ 1.$$

It is perhaps interesting to visualize an example of different modes of definition of isometric subdivisions. Consider, in our model, subdivisions characterized by (1) shape, (2) material and (3) surface color. Such a subdivision might be exemplified by spheres made of gold with surface color red. Here $j = 3$ and $j! = 6$. Consequently the subdivisions in question could be defined by the following six hierarchial arrangements of the three sets of categories.

	Shape		Shape		Color		Color
(1)	Material	(2)	Color	(3)	Shape	(4)	Material
	Color		Material		Material		Shape

	Material		Material
(5)	Color	(6)	Shape
	Shape		Color

Hierarchial order (1) would provide no subdivision for all objects made from a given material and having a given surface color, thus no subdivision is provided for red objects made from gold as would, however, be the case with hierarchial orders (4) and (5). This illustrates the important fact that different modes of definition of isometric subdivisions at one level, (here the third) can generate certain isometrically distinct and also isometrically identical subdivisions at other levels.

It will be recalled that the classification systems that we have been considering are built up of subdivisions each of which is defined in terms of a combination of characteristics with each combination containing no more than one characteristic from any one of the sets into which the characteristics are organized. In somewhat more formal language, all the subdivisions of the classification systems are built up by establishing logical products of characteristics taken from sets of mutually exclusive characteristics. It is perhaps obvious that such classification systems constitute a special type. The more general types of system would include subdivisions defined not only in terms of logical products but also logical sums and logical differences. Hence, our mathematical analysis of our model system must be regarded as capable of considerable

extension. Nevertheless, the mathematical analysis presented in previous paragraphs suffices to establish points of
decisive importance in planning applications of various systems and equipment. These points are best made by considering how our mathematical model provides a common basis
for understanding the capabilities and limitations of several
forms of documentation systems, especially compartmentalized classification, alphabetized index (and similar systems
based on ordered arrays), systems (e. g. the Universal Decimal Classification) that characterize documents in terms of
one or a multiplicity of classification numbers, aspect systems such as Batten, Peek-a-boo or Uniterm, coding systems
for use with hand-sorted punched cards or with more versatile
searching and selecting equipment.

D.   Classification and Definition of Concepts and Terminology

     In order that our mathematical model may be of greatest
help to us in conducting a review of methods and systems, it
is necessary to take note of the close relationships between
(1) definition of classes and subclasses in a classification system and (2) the definition of concepts and of terminology used
to express and record concepts. These relationships are
perhaps most obvious in the field of taxonomy. For example,
the term "fish" refers to animals having certain characteristics.
The same is true not only of the full range of terminology used in
taxonomy, such as coelenterate, parnassia, but also of such
everyday concepts and words, as tree, house, chair, shirt,
etc. With everyday words, the sharpness of definition may be
less than with terminology subject to scientific control. Such
lack of precision in the definition of many concepts and words
is, of course, a factor that requires consideration when conducting such operations as indexing, classifying and coding
information for machine searching. Even when a tolerable
level of precision in definition is attained, we observe that
words vary in scope of meaning. For example, "animal",
"mammal", "dog", "fish", "bird", and "tree" all refer to
living organisms but to different sets or groups of the same.
Further, we observe that there is a tendency for words to
overlap in meaning (more or less near synonyms). These
factors must be taken into account in constructing classification systems, indexes, codes for machine searching and

similar systems for analyzing information and facilitating its
retrieval, correlation and utilization.

(1) Use of Characteristics in Definitions

Let us start our review of the formulation of concepts and
the definition of terminology by observing that any set of characteristics may be used to define a concept and a word to
denote the concept in question. Thus, it might be imagined
that, in some prehistoric civilization, gold spheres four inches
in diameter may have had some unusual significance, perhaps
of a religious nature. If this were the case, then it is virtually certain that a special word, e.g., ishker, would be used
to designate such objects. The point being emphasized is that
any combination of characteristics - no matter how arbitrary
such a combination may appear - may be used to formulate a
concept and to define a corresponding word.

The formulation of concepts and the definition of terminology as observed in human languages are controlled in part
by environment but more especially by human response to
events, observations and experiences. In so far as our everyday language is concerned, we are strongly influenced by the
lengthy accumulated experience of our ancestors. There can
be little doubt that intuitive factors were of determining importance in establishing the basic concepts of our language and
in the evolution of many of those words in general and frequent
use that form the basic framework of our language. In our
industrial civilization, many of us have frequent occasion to
make use of concepts and terminology whose formulation and
definition have been accomplished, in large measure at least,
on the basis of the analytical procedures of scientific observation and those generalizing-synthesizing correlations that
are scientific hypotheses, theories and laws of nature.

Concepts and terminology are thus both the product of
human efforts to cope with the environment and also tools used
as aids in such efforts. In some instances, it is easy to understand why certain words are used in a specific language. For
example, it is easy to understand why the Eskimo language has
specific individual words for different types of snow which we
might describe, perhaps, as powdery snow, compacted snow,
granular snow. These Eskimo words may be regarded as near

synonyms for which we have the single generic term, "snow",
which may be used in conjunction with a qualifier to refer to
a particular type of snow. Note in this connection that we have
different words for ice, snow and water which are all different
physical forms of the same chemical substance. The language
of a tropical primitive tribe whose ancestral experiences have
never involved ice can be expected to be forced to describe ice
as "cold solid water" in much the same way that we must describe a form of snow for which the Eskimo language has a
separate word.

In some realms of language, particularly scientific and
technical terminology, the very structure of words suggests
certain more basic concepts, e. g., thermometer suggests
"heat measure", phonograph suggests "sound write", etc. A
majority of terms, including many of scientific and technical
character, cannot be so easily and obviously related to more
basic concepts. Even when the relationship between specific
terms and more generic concepts is apparent from their ety-
mology, there is no one basic set of concepts that is used in a
consistent fashion for word derivation. In fact even those concepts or terms of more generic character can be analyzed in
terms of other general ideas. The formulation of concepts and
the definition of terms is such that the attempt to arrive at
their formulation in terms of logical absolutes leads eventually
to such concepts as "and", "not", "there exists". The extreme-
ly abstract nature of these concepts makes them ineffective
as the basis for analyzing the information in documents and for
conducting searching, selecting and correlating operations.
Expression of the characteristics of the objects in our mathematical model in terms of logical absolutes would be a difficult and impractical tour de force.

Instead of logical absolutes, the conceptual framework of
language in general, and of science and technology in particular, consists of a multiplicity of interrelated ideas and related
terms. Some are of broader scope than others and there is
often considerable overlap in scope of meaning. Providing
measures for degree of generic character and for extent of
synonymous overlap would require that we establish a set of
basic concepts whose relationships with other concepts and
terms would then have to be investigated. Accomplishing such

a program would involve considerable effort and in any case is outside the scope of this book.

(2) <u>Measuring Degree of Generality and Synonymity</u>

Our mathematical model enables us, however, to indicate how we might proceed in developing measures for degree of generic character and for degree of synonymity. It will be recalled that our mathematical model is based on ten sets of characteristics. (See Figure 1.) The number of characteristics is ten in each of five of the sets, 26 in two sets and 100 in three sets. As noted in previous discussion, these basic characteristics may be combined in various ways to generate derived characteristics. For both the basic characteristics and also for the derived characteristics we might measure degree of generic character and degree of synonymity as follows. Two characteristics would be said to be equal in generic character if they pertain to the same number of objects in our model system. Thus, the characteristic "sphere" and the Roman numeral "IV" would be equally generic in our system. A derived characteristic, such as "sphere" with Roman numeral "IV", would pertain to only one-tenth as many objects and consequently this derived characteristic would be only one-tenth as generic in character as its parent basic characteristics.

Thus we might establish a measure of the degree to which a given characteristic, either basic or derived, is generic in nature by the formula:

$$D_G = \frac{N'}{N_\Sigma}$$

where D_G = degree of generic character, N' = number of objects to which a given characteristic applies, N_Σ = total number of objects embraced by the system.

The above definition also points the way to measuring the relative degree of generic character of two characteristics. The more generic term would have a larger value of D_G and the relative degree of generic character might be computed as the ratio of the values of D_G for the two characteristics in question.

In our mathematical model the basic characteristics

within a single set are in no way or degree synonymous. For
example, the basic characteristic "sphere" applies to none of
the objects to which the characteristic "truncated cone" applies. Furthermore, since we have stipulated that, in our
model system, each object may be marked by only one capital
letter, the basic characteristic "D" is also in no way synonymous with the basic characteristic "N". The degree of synonymity would be complete for derived characteristics defined
by means of the same basic characteristics with the further
stipulation that the latter stand in the same relationships in
the definition of the derived characteristics. In other words,
the isometrically equivalent definitions of subdivisions, each
of which embrace the same set of objects, may be considered
to also define a corresponding set of completely synonymous
derived characteristics. Our discussion of classification
systems based on the logical product relationship provided
some simple examples of such completely synonymous derived
characteristics. Other types of more or less synonymous derived characteristics might be defined by making use of the
relationships of logical sum and logical difference as previously discussed. The degree of synonymity between two terms
might be defined, with reference to our mathematical model
as follows:

$$D_s = \frac{N_b}{(\frac{N_I + N_{II}}{2})}$$

where D_s = degree of synonymity, N_b = number of objects to
which both terms apply, N_I = number of objects to which the
first of the two terms apply, N_{II} = number of objects to which
the second of the two terms apply.

These definitions of degree of generic character and of
degree of synonymity are based, it should be emphasized, on
our mathematical model. Nevertheless, by establishing an
approach to evaluating generic character and synonymity the
above discussed definitions facilitate greatly subsequent discussion of various forms of clasifying, indexing and coding for
machine or manual searching. It is not intended to imply in
such discussion that the above presented definitions, established on the basis of a closed system, are immediately and
directly applicable to all situations encountered in practice.

It is intended, however, that these definitions shall serve to make the concepts of generic character and synonymity easier to understand, less nebulous and consequently more useful when designing information systems. In particular, these definitions serve to emphasize the close relationship between classifying objects and referring to them by using terminology of more or less generic character. From a generalized point of view we may regard the numbers used to designate the subdivisions in classification systems as specially defined terminology of more or less generic character. Some classification systems, e.g. the Universal Decimal Classification, are so established that a considerable degree of synonymity may exist between different classification subdivisions.

We might summarize this part of our discussion with the statement that to speak of things has much in common with classifying them and to classify things has much in common with speaking of them.

CHAPTER III

SELECTIVITY CRITERIA FOR SYSTEMS EVALUATION

A. Introduction

The mathematical model presented in the preceding chapter could be applied to the analysis of any system for accomplishing selecting, grouping and classifying operations regardless of whether we are concerned with nuts and bolts, kitchen utensils, children's play things--or written records of professional interest.

The present chapter has two purposes. One is to present a rather general discussion of the importance of class definition and related identifying and selecting operations when making use of extensive files of graphic records. The other purpose is to summarize certain criteria for evaluating the performance and reliability of systems for identifying and selecting graphic records of pertinent interest to a given problem or situation.

We shall assume a collection of graphic records (reports, patents, papers, drawings, photographs, etc.) numbering N_Σ at any time, t. We shall assume that only a part of these are of interest to a given problem or situation that arises at time, t. The number of items of pertinent interest to a given problem or situation, we shall designate by x. Then by assumption and definition:

$$\frac{x}{N_\Sigma} < 1$$

Consideration of the magnitude of this fraction enables us to specify what we mean by a "more generic search" or a "more specific search". One search is more generic than another, when x/N_Σ is greater. Evaluation of x/N_Σ for different searches permits the relative terms "generic" and "specific" to be brought within the realm of measurement and also related to our mathematical model. Thus we define f_g, the generic factor, equal to x/n_Σ

26

B. Criteria of Selectivity

For the frequently encountered situation that $\frac{x}{N_\Sigma}$ is a
small fraction, it is advantageous to provide some system
that permits the totality of records, N_Σ, to be divided into two
parts, without necessity of personal inspection of each item
in the collection. This system may be set up in many different ways. But regardless of the design, the purpose is always
the same. To arrive at a division of the file so that the selected items, to be denoted by m, are the same, or at least
include, those items, x, of pertinent interest to a given problem or situation. Thus operation of the system must be judged
on the basis of the following factors:

1. Value of the recall factor, f_r -

   $f_r = w/x$

   where w is number of items within m
   that are of pertinent interest

2. Value of the pertinency factor f_p -

   $f_p = \frac{w}{m}$

3. Value of the resolution factor, f_{rs} -

   $f_{rs} = \frac{m}{n_\Sigma}$

4. Value of the omission factor, f_{om} -

   $f_{om} = \frac{x-w}{x}$

5. Value of the noise factor, f_n -

   $f_n = \frac{m-w}{m}$

When it is important, as is often the case, that attention
be directed to as large a fraction of pertinent items as may be
possible or practical from the systems cost point of view, then
w/x must be as near unity as possible. To reduce the number
of items that must be eliminated by personal inspection--
always an expensive operation--it is important that w/m also
be near unity. When $f_r = 1$, then $f_{om} = 0$ and when $f_p = 1$,
then $f_n = 0$. Thus the omission factor and the noise factor may
be regarded as alternate ways of stating the recall factor and
the pertinency factor.

Figures 3-8 show how varying values of m, x and w may interact to provide varying combinations of values for f_r, f_p, f_{rs}, f_{om}, f_n and f_g.

It should be emphasized that the definition of various factors, and also the Figures used to illustrate some of the relationships that may be observed to exist between them, may be considered to indicate the results obtained by a single operation of a given system. As time passes both the system and the information requirements may undergo change. Thus with passage of time, new items will enter the system and some of these items may pertain to subjects that are new in nature. Changes in information requirements may result from new problems and situations. Such changes--or at least their possibility--must be taken into account when designing a system and when evaluating its effectiveness.

At any given time (i.e. at the corresponding stage in the evolution of a collection of items), different searches can be expected to provide different values of w, m and x, also different values of the factors, f_r, f_p, f_{rs}, f_{om} and f_n. For a number of searches, e.g. 100, distribution curves, such as those shown in Figure 9, may be observed for f_r or f_p. Here the more sharply peaked curves would indicate a greater uniformity of performance for different searches. Departure of such curves from the shapes shown in Figure 9 may provide the basis for diagnosing weaknesses in a given system. For examples of such departure, see Figure 10. Comparison of such curves provide means for evaluating the performance of different systems and the changing performance of a system as it undergoes changes with the passage of time or as demands made on the system change with time.

C. Cost Considerations

In considering the evaluation of systems, it is advisable to take into account the fact that, for identical curves of shape illustrated in Figure 9, the satisfactory or unsatisfactory evaluation of a system may be strongly influenced by different values of N_Σ (number of items in file). If x/N_Σ remains constant as well as m/N_Σ and w/m for different values of N_Σ then the number of non-pertinent items, namely m-w, will increase proportionately to N_Σ, so also will the number of pertinent

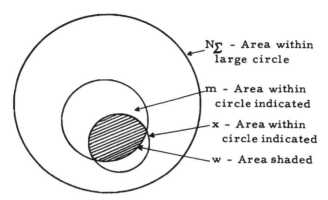

Figure 3.

$f_r = w/x$ - Fairly large; $f_p = w/m$ - Fairly large

$f_{om} = \frac{x-w}{x}$ - Fairly low; $f_n = \frac{m-w}{m}$ - Fairly low

Situation provides opportunity for improvement.

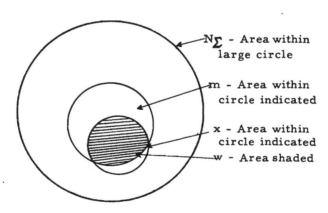

Figure 4.

More favorable values of f_r, f_p, f_{om}, f_m than in Figure 3, but same values of m and x.

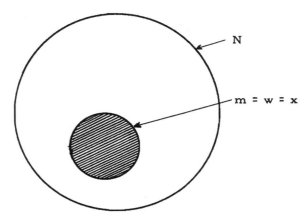

Figure 5
Ideal situation with m = w = x
and f_r as well as f_p = 1
f_{om} as well as f_n = 0

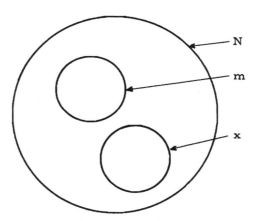

Figure 6
Completely unfavorable situation
with w = o
f_r and f_p = 0
f_{om} and f_n = 1

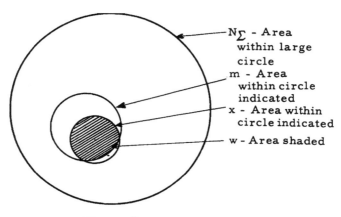

Figure 7

Situation with same values for N_Σ and m as in Figures 3 and 4 but smaller value of x.

(Note that this figure also provides opportunity for improvement ment)

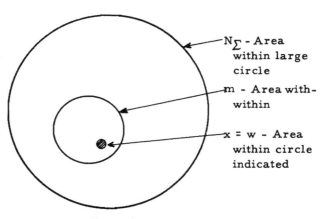

Figure 8

Situation favorable for recall factor ($f_r = 1$) but unfavorable with regard to f_p (low pertinency factor). Note favorable f_{om} but unfavorable f_n.

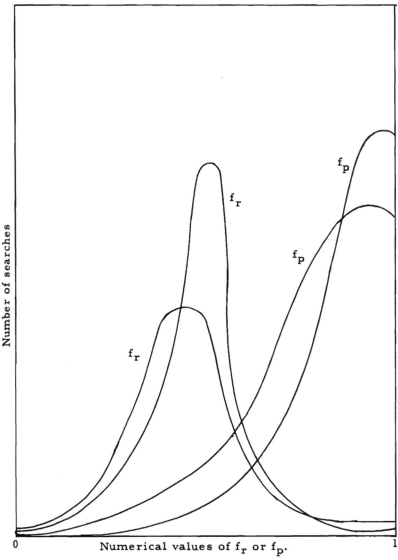

Figure 9.

Distribution Curves for f_r and f_p for Different
Searches Performed with Two Different Systems

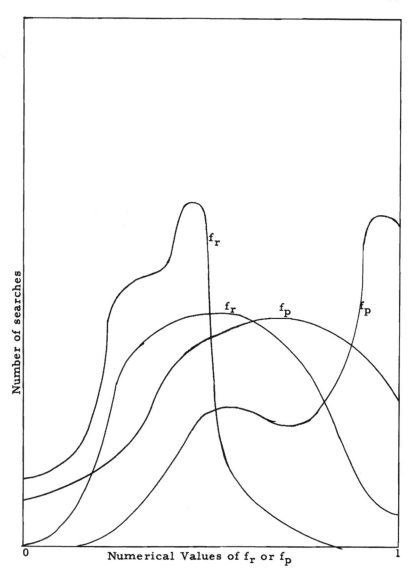

Figure 10.
Distribution Curves for f_r and f_p for Sets of
Searches Performed either with Different
Systems or with Same System at Different
Stages of Evolution

items to which the system failed to direct attention. This
latter number of overlooked items is indicated by x-w. Figure
11 shows graphs illustrating these points. Note that the slopes
of such lines will depend on the manner of graduation of the
ordinate and abscissa and also the values of m-w and x-w at
the initial conditions, $N_\Sigma = N_o$ at t_o. Such increase in x-w
would result in more information being overlooked with the
larger file. Increase in m-w would result in corresponding
effort being devoted to personal review of material of no interest. Such cost, denoted by s_{ni}, during a time interval while
N_Σ and m-w remains substantially unchanged would be--

$$s_{ni} = k_3 \, d(m-w)$$

where k_3 = cost of considering a
single document
d = number of searches
during the time interval

If $\dfrac{dN_\Sigma}{dt} = a$ where a is a constant

then at any time, t, --

$$m - w = \frac{(m-w)_o}{N_o} \, N_\Sigma$$

where $(m-w)_o$ is the value of m-w
at N_o and t_o

Furthermore --

$$N_\Sigma = N_o + at$$

if, as assumed, $\dfrac{dN_\Sigma}{dt} = a$

Then

$$s_{ni} = k_3 d \, \frac{(m-w)_o}{N_o} \, (N_o + at)$$

Since s_{ni}, by definition, is cost per time interval --

$$\frac{d(\Sigma S_{ni})}{dt} = s_{ni}$$

where ΣS_{ni} is the summation of
this cost at time, t.

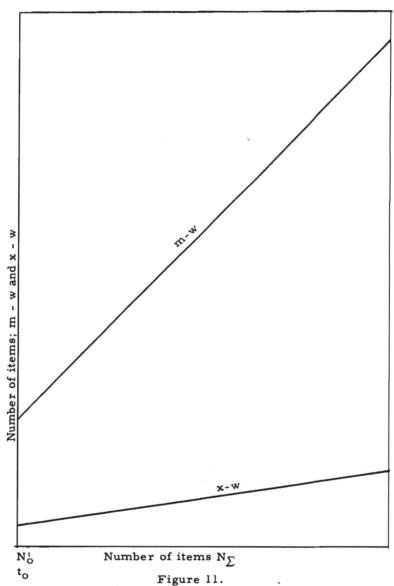

Figure 11.
Graphs Illustrating Changes in Extraneous Items (m - w) and
Items Missed (x - w) with Increasing Size of File

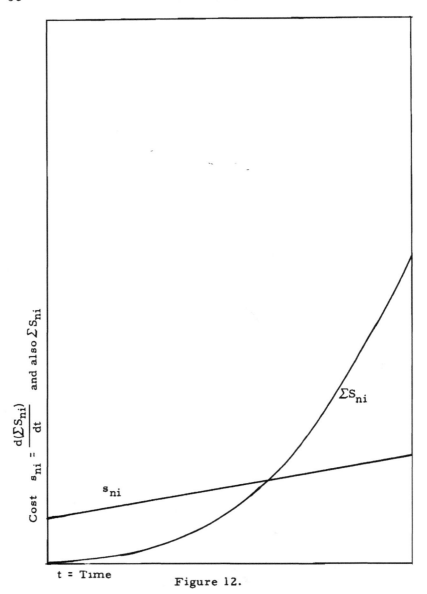

Figure 12.

Cost per Unit Time and Cumulated Cost of Personal
Review of Non-pertinent Documents

$$\frac{d(\Sigma S_{ni})}{dt} = k_3 d \frac{(m-w)_o}{N_o} (N_o + at)$$

$$\Sigma S_{ni} = k_3 d (m-w)_o t + \frac{k_3 d (m-w)_o}{N_o} at^2$$

Graphs illustrating s_{ni} and ΣS_{ni} as functions of time are shown in Figure 12.

The cost, s_{ni}, can easily become a decisive factor in annual budgeting for information systems. The cumulative cost ΣS_{ni}, can also become a factor justifying a considerable initial investment that may be effective in permitting a reduction in $(m-w)_o$ and also in m-w at later times.

D. Summary

A consideration of purposes to be served by selection operations involving large collections of graphic records leads to the following conclusions:

The basic requirement is to provide the capability of eliminating from consideration items that are irrelevant to a given problem or situation.

This basic requirement is closely related to a second requirement, namely the ability to select out and draw together items of pertinent interest.

Fulfillment of the first requirement but not the second implies placing limits on the range of requirements that the system may serve at reasonable cost. These limits may rule out servicing information requirements of various types (narrow specific searches, broad generic searches) depending on the factors that establish the limits.

A third requirement is for reliability of operation. Here the decisive questions are:

What benefits are lost; what expenses are incurred, when, in a given search, information is not retrieved? To what extent are greater costs for information systems justified to provide more reliable results?

CHAPTER IV

ANALYSIS OF COST FACTORS

A. Introduction

Previous chapters have been concerned with certain principles of basic importance to the definition of purposes to be served by documentation systems and to the evaluation of their performance and effectiveness. In meeting practical situations, it must be kept in mind that recent technological advances, particularly in electronics, are making available equipment that differs so greatly from traditional library devices, both as to capabilities already achieved and future potentialities, that considerable imagination may be required to visualize and to achieve potential advantages. This section is written to serve two purposes: (1) to indicate how possible applications of newly available equipment may be evaluated on an engineering basis; and (2) to indicate relationships between cost factors and limitations of conventional indexing and classifying methods and thus to stimulate imaginative thinking as to ways of applying newly available equipment to specific situations.

The approach in this section is to present a mathematical analysis of various operations involved in using recorded information. In carrying through this analysis, particular attention has been directed to: (1) costs of processing information; and (2) costs of conducting searches and achieving correlations when information is processed in various ways. Specifically, attention is directed to the following topics:

> Storage of Graphic Records
> Compartmentalized Classification
> Alphabetized Indexing

Each topic is treated independently but with the same symbols being used for all topics.

The derivation of the various equations assumes no mathematical knowledge beyond the undergraduate engineering level. All the more important equations are illustrated by typical graphs to assist in visualizing cost trends and similar relationships. In considering these graphs, it must be kept in mind that they are merely illustrative. The shape and position of curves corresponding to an actual situation would depend on the parameters specific to a given situation. Hence in arriving at conclusions with regard to a given situation, the equations must provide guidance rather than the accompanying illustrative graphs.

B. Storage of Graphic Records

Let us consider a file of graphic records into which new items are being entered and from which older items are being discarded. For purposes of deriving equations and establishing relationships, we shall define the following quantities:

N_Σ = number of items in file at any time, t.
t = time
t_o = starting time
b = number of items in file at starting time, t_o
b_1, b_2, b_3 = specific values of b at time t_1, t_2, t_3
a = number of items entering file per unit time, (which might, for individual cases, be taken differently) e. g. a year.
a_1, a_2, a_3 = specific values of a in specific situations.
c = number of items discarded from the file per unit time.
c_1, c_2, c_3 = specific values of c in specific situations.
$a - c = A$ = net increase in number of items in the file per unit time.

It is perhaps immediately obvious that the quantities a, c and A may all be functions of time. The simplest relationship between A and t is that A does not change with t or, in other words, A is a constant with time. It is to this simple case that we shall direct attention. For more complex functions, the equations as derived below would, of course, turn out differently. But even in such cases, the same general line of reasoning as to cost factors would apply and such reasoning would guide the derivation of more complex equations.

If we assume A to be a constant with respect to time, then in the language of differential equations

$$\frac{dN_\Sigma}{dt} = A = a \text{ constant}$$

Integrating we have

$$N_\Sigma = At + b \qquad\qquad (1)$$

where, as stated above,

        b = number of items initially in the file

        A = net rate of accession of items into the file·

Equation (1) determines a straight line on ordinary orthogonal coordinates. The position and shape of the line will be determined by the values of A and b in conjunction with the scales for the ordinate and absissca. Thus in Figure 13, the line indicated by the numeral 1 corresponds to the case that A = 0, that is, a file with no new documents entering it. Line 2 illustrates the situation for a file of considerable size at the start (time, t_o) but with slow growth. Line 3 shows the growth of a file having a small number of items at time zero but with a larger value of growth rate, A, than was the case for line 2. An intermediate situation between the situations represented by the lines 2 and 3 is shown by line 4. The values for both of the constants A and b are intermediate between those for the two lines 2 and 3.

The cost of storing a collection of graphic records may be divided into two kinds:

(1) Not caused by storage space requirements -

      s_1 = first kind of costs (e.g. personnel, overhead, filing costs) per unit of time, e.g., per year

      s_o = amount of s_1 cost when N_Σ = 0

      k_1 = increment in s_1 costs/item in file

For a given time unit (e.g., per year)

$$s_1 = k_1 N_\Sigma + s_o$$

(2) Caused by storage space requirements

      s_2 = second kind of costs per unit, e.g., annual rent of storage space

      k_2 = increment in s_2 costs/item in file

For a given time unit (e.g., per year)

$$s_2 = k_2 N_\Sigma$$

Overall cost, S, per unit time is the sum of these two

$$S = s_1 + s_2 = k_1 N_\Sigma + s_o + k_2 N_\Sigma$$

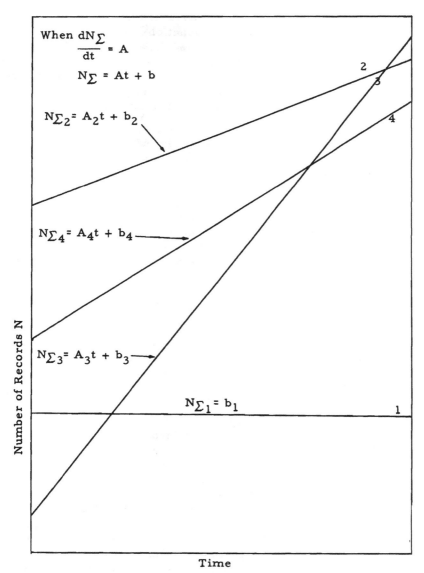

When $\dfrac{dN_\Sigma}{dt} = A$

$N_\Sigma = At + b$

$N_{\Sigma_2} = A_2 t + b_2$

$N_{\Sigma_4} = A_4 t + b_4$

$N_{\Sigma_3} = A_3 t + b_3$

$N_{\Sigma_1} = b_1$

Number of Records N

Time

Figure 13.

Growth of a File of Records.

Note that both k_1 and k_2 are assumed to be constant with respect to N_Σ. If k_1 and k_2 are functions of N_Σ, the analysis would be rendered more complicated. (Parenthetically, it is known that in traditional library systems unit costs for filing, shelving and servicing do increase with increase in the size of the collection, but for the sake of simplicity in a first formulation the assumption that they are constant seems justified.)

The relationship between the above mentioned two kinds of costs can be expected to be strongly influenced by the storage methods used. If methods are not employed to keep down storage space requirements, then costs for storage space (type 2 costs) may be found in a given case to rise more rapidly as the file expands than do the other (type 1) costs. Such a case is illustrated by Figure 14. Here the type 1 constants, shown by line 1, increase slowly with time while costs for storage space, as shown by line 2, increase more rapidly. Total costs, shown by line 3, are the sum of the two types of costs shown by lines 1 and 2. Each of these lines represents costs for the time unit selected to analyze a given situation. Thus the costs as shown in Figure 14 might be computed on an annual basis.

Since we are assuming a direct proportionality between the two types of storage costs and the number of documents, there is also a direct proportionality between the total costs and the number of documents. The equation of the total cost line may be rewritten as

$$S = k_1 N_\Sigma + k_2 N_\Sigma + s_0$$

Here s_0 may be thought of as costs involved in maintaining an establishment of minimum storage capacity but including such necessities as a clerical staff, etc., that must be provided when the collection is of negligible size. k_1 when multiplied by N_Σ (line 1 in Figure 14) will show how these relatively fixed costs may tend to rise slowly as a document collection expands. Line 2 in Figure 14 indicates increasing costs required for warehousing, that is to say, for storage space. Note here the importance of the proportionality constant k_2 which indicated the cost for storage space per document. Finally, as already note, line 3 represents a summation of these two types of costs. It should be emphasized that the costs shown in Figure 14 all pertain to costs per unit time, for example, the cost

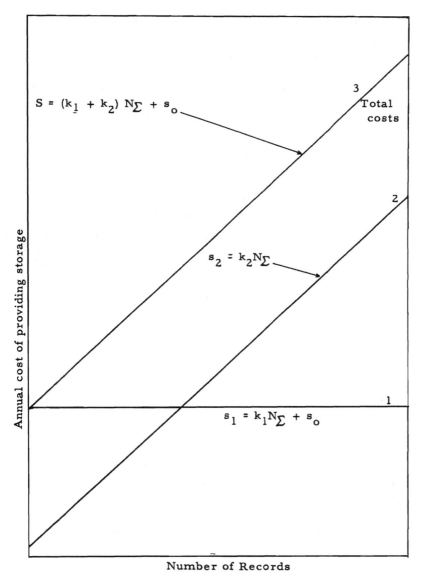

$$S = (k_1 + k_2) N_\Sigma + s_o$$

3
Total costs

$$s_2 = k_2 N_\Sigma$$

2

1

$$s_1 = k_1 N_\Sigma + s_o$$

Annual cost of providing storage

Number of Records

Figure 14.

Increase in annual cost of storing records as file expands.

incurred per year for records in a given file.

Consideration of annual costs is, however, only a part of the story, although it is obviously an important one to which we will return after considering another important aspect of the storage cost situation, namely the cumulation of costs year after year. Thus, we might denote cumulated costs by ΣS which after the x - th year (or other time period) would be given by the equation:

$$\Sigma S = S_1 + S_2 + S_3 + S_4 + -- S_x$$

where S_1 = total costs for the first year

S_2 = total costs for the second year

etc., and

S_x = total costs for the x - th year

and thus compute the cost for x years. If now we undertake to show by graphs how the cumulated costs ΣS, change with time, it is perhaps immediately apparent that the increment in ΣS for a given time unit, such as a year, is equal to the annual cost, or in the language of the differential calculus:

$$\frac{d\Sigma S}{dt} = S$$

Next, in accord with the previous derivations, we recall that:

$$S = (k_1 + k_2) N_\Sigma + s_o$$

and furthermore that

$$N_\Sigma = At + b$$

On making the obvious substitutions, we arrive at the equation

$$\frac{d\Sigma S}{dt} = (k_1 + k_2) (At + b) + s_o$$

Integrating, we find that:

$$\Sigma S = (k_1 + k_2) (\frac{A}{2} t^2) + (k_1 + k_2) (bt) + s_o t + C$$

where C is the constant of integration and here represents those cost factors incurred prior to time, t_o, in setting up the record storage operation. This equation permits us to separate costs into three categories to be designated by ΣS_1, ΣS_2 and ΣS_3 as follows:

<u>First category</u> - Cumulated annual costs not caused by storage space requirements.

$$\Sigma S_1 = k_1 (\frac{At^2}{2} + bt) + s_o t$$

Second category - Cumulated annual costs caused by
storage space requirements.

$$\Sigma S_2 = k_2 \left(\frac{At^2}{2} + bt \right)$$

Third category - Initial costs when establishing the storage
system prior to t_o.

$$\Sigma S_3 = C$$

Consideration of these three cost categories and relationships between them can provide the basis for deciding whether,
as far as storage costs are concerned, it will be advantageous
or not to apply a given system or machine in a given situation.
To illustrate both the performance and the results of such analysis, Figures 15 through 20 are presented.

Figure 15 has the purpose of indicating how the various
cost factors ΣS_1, ΣS_2 and ΣS_3 may be considered separately
and how the addition of these three factors yields the total
cumulated cost, ΣS.

Interactions between these three types of costs are particularly important to evaluating possibilities of applying given
systems or equipment. Let us consider first a situation in
which ΣS_3 is virtually eliminated. In other words, a record
storage facility is set up so as to make the minimum investment in storage means or equipment for facilitating storage
(See Figure 16.) Such an arrangement might be exemplified by
a record storage unit in which office space and storage space
are rented as required and a small permanent staff is hired.
The cost of office space and the permanent staff would then be
represented by ΣS_1 and the expanding cost for greater and
greater amount of record storage room would correspond to
ΣS_2. This certainly corresponds to a situation in which the
annual storage costs start out at a low level but, because of
continuing rather rapid increase in storage costs (see line 2
in Figure 14), the annual costs tend to increase steadily. Cumulated costs for such a situation are illustrated by Figure 16.
It is evident, however, from Figure 16 that as time goes on a
larger and larger amount of money continues to be spent for
rental of storage space as is shown by the curve ΣS_2. The
question arises whether the rental of storage space is the most
efficient way to make use of this money. As shown in Figure 16,

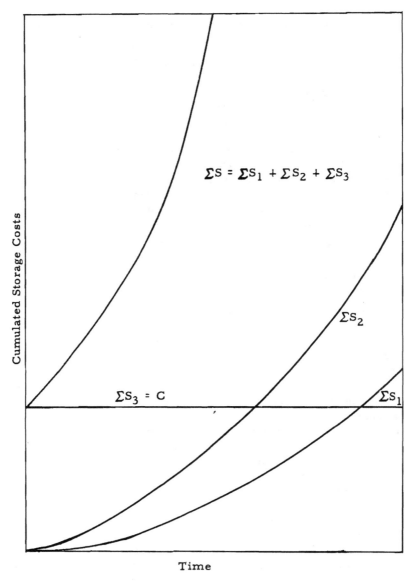

$$\Sigma S = \Sigma S_1 + \Sigma S_2 + \Sigma S_3$$

ΣS_2

$\Sigma S_3 = C$

ΣS_1

Time

Figure 15.

Cumulated storage costs vs. time.

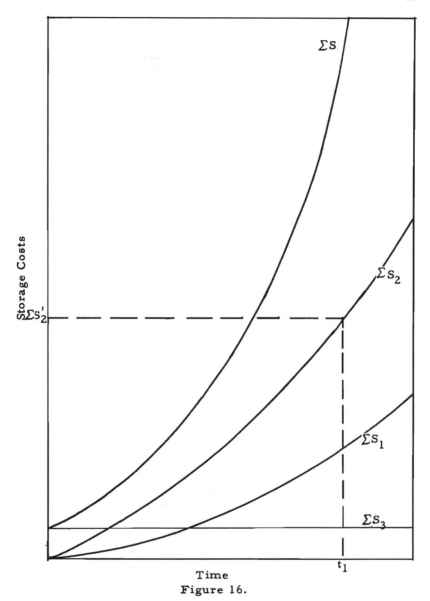

Time

Figure 16.

Cumulated storage costs vs time (when ΣS_3 is low)

at a certain time t_1, the total cumulated costs for storage
space would be represented by $\Sigma S_2'$. Let us now investigate
how the situation might be altered if a large fraction of the
sum represented by $\Sigma S_2'$ has been invested in equipment which
would have reduced drastically the volume of storage space.
Once this investment has been made, the annual cost situation
would change as shown in Figure 17 which is, as will be immediately apparent, a redrawing of Figure 16, but with a
greatly reduced value for the coefficient k_2. The initial equipment has prevented a rapid rise in s_2, the annual costs shown
in Figure 17. As a consequence the total annual costs shown
in Figure 17 are much lower than the corresponding costs
shown in Figure 16. On the other hand, it must be kept in
mind that this favorable effect on annual costs required a considerable initial investment which must find its justification
in terms of eventual savings over a period of years. To indicate how such justification may be demonstrated let us redraw
Figure 16 with a rather large initial investment indicated by
ΣS_3 at time t_o and let us assume further that this investment
is indeed effective in lowering the annual storage cost as
shown in Figure 17. Then the picture of cumulated costs
might be exemplified by Figure 18. Here, due to the large
initial investment, cumulated costs are at first higher than in
Figure 16. Thanks to the slower rate with which cumulated
costs build up in Figure 18, these costs, after passing a certain point in time, are below the level shown in Figure 16. In
fact, from then on, the differences in total cumulated costs
between Figures 16 and 18 become increasingly in favor of
Figure 18. To emphasize this important point, Figure 19 has
been prepared. As this Figure shows, up to time, t_1, the total
cumulated costs shown in Figure 18 are greater than the total
cumulated costs shown in Figure 16. During this time period,
the situation might be summarized by saying that the initial
equipment investment--the ΣS_3 factor--overshadows the savings which the initial investment makes possible. From time
t_1 onward, however, these savings more than compensate for
the initial investment in equipment and, in fact, from t_1 onward the spread between the two curves becomes greater and
greater indicating a continuingly greater cumulated saving year
after year. It is perhaps well to emphasize also that not only
do the cumulated savings become greater, but the annual oper-

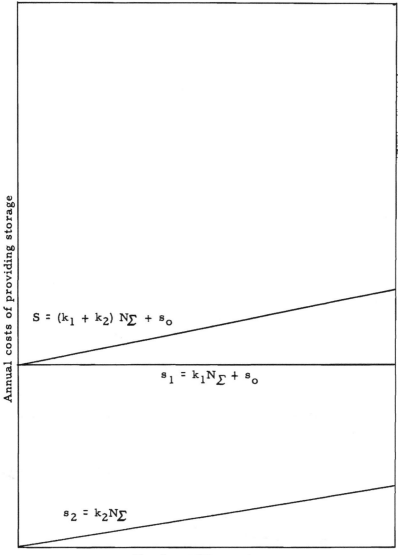

Number of Records
Figure 17.

Lowering of annual costs by decreasing space requirements for storage.

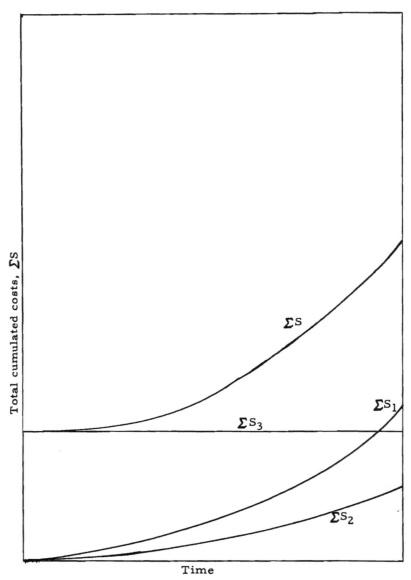

Figure 18.

Cumulated storage costs when investment in equipment greatly lowers storage space requirements.

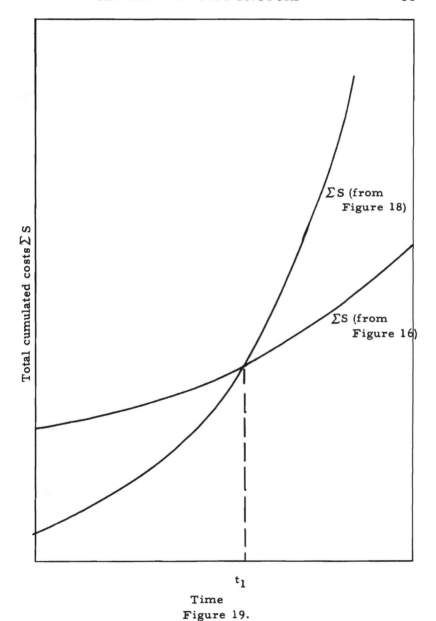

Time

Figure 19.

Economies achieved after time, t_1, by initial investment to reduce space requirements.

ating costs are also held at a lower level. This becomes evident on comparing, as has been done in Figure 20, the annual total costs shown in Figures 16 and 17.

In our analysis of the cost situation with respect to storage of document collections, certain simplifying assumptions have been made. Perhaps the most important of these is linear proportionality between the number of documents in a file and time, or, in less mathematical language, we have assumed that the rate of growth of the file is a constant. It is observed with many files that their rate of growth increases with time. In other words instead of:

$$\frac{dN_\Sigma}{dt} = A = \text{a constant}$$

we have:

$$\frac{dN_\Sigma}{dt} = f(t)$$

where in many practical situations f (t) may be represented reasonably accurately by a power series. In other words, in many practical situations:

$$\frac{dN_\Sigma}{dt} = a' + b't + c't^2 + d't^3 \text{ ---}$$

If such dependence of rate of file growth were taken into account, there would be considerable changes in the equations derived. However, the course of derivation would not be changed nor would the character of the conclusions be altered. In other words, our general approach to analyzing storage costs to determine when application of given systems or equipment may be justified would remain substantially unchanged.

The graphs presented in Figures 13-20 inclusive provide specific illustrations of situations in which various constants, especially A, b, s_o, k_1, k_2 have been assumed to have certain numerical values. The various curves and their shapes depend, of course, on the values of such constants, which must be determined by an actual survey of the conditions under which a given file operates. It must be emphasized that it is the application of the equations after determination of the various parameters in a situation which will provide the basis for deciding whether or not given systems or equipment are appropriate for application in a given situation.

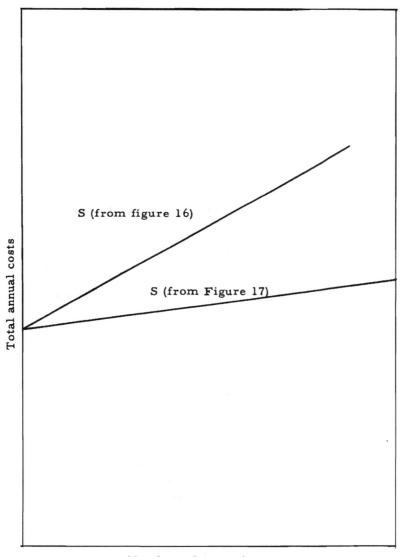

Figure 20.

Reduction in annual operating costs by reduction in
space requirements achieved by initial investment.

C. Compartmentalized Classification

(1) Introductory Notes

In many situations in which we find it necessary to deal with a large number of individual objects, their grouping into sets is highly convenient and useful. The housewife, for example, groups her tableware and kitchen utensils so that plates of different sizes, knives, forks, spoons, etc., are conveniently at hand. In the stockroom of a chemical laboratory, a similar grouping or classification facilitates the location of such items as test tubes, beakers, Erlenmeyer flasks or stoppers. For many years, the patent offices of the world--with a few notable exceptions--have relied on the grouping of their patent specifications into a predetermined array of classes and subclasses to make it possible, at reasonable cost, to identify those previously issued patents whose subject matter may be of pertinent interest to a newly filed application for patent. It is highly desirable, in the interest of industrial progress, that patents shall be issued only for inventions that are actually new and not already described in previously issued patents or other earlier publications.

It is perhaps immediately apparent that the grouping of documents or other items into a fixed array depends for its success on several conditions, of which the following are particularly important:

(1) The range of subject matter included in each item must not be so broad as to require its classification into more than a reasonable number of subclasses. Here the key word is "reasonable" and its interpretation, in the light of costs and benefits, depends on various circumstances as considered subsequently.

(2) The amount of time and effort required to conduct a search must be kept within reasonable limits. It is particularly advantageous to be able to conduct a complete search by considering items classified in a single subclass. It is, furthermore, advantageous if each grouping contains a sufficiently small number of items that their personal inspection does not impose a burdensome task. Conversely, a compartmentalized classification system must be regarded as less and less satisfactory as the probability increases that a

given search will require that the items in a multiplicity of subclasses will have to be reviewed either
by the person requiring information or by someone
else having expert knowledge of the subject matter.

At one time these conditions appear to have been reasonably well met in so far as the search requirements of the U. S.
Patent Office are concerned. With the evolution of modern technology, the number of issued patents has increased greatly,
with nearly 2,000,000 U. S. patents being issued since the turn
of the century. It has become necessary to provide many new
subclasses to prevent overcrowding of previous classes. Accomplishing this task in such a way as to continue to satisfy
the two requirements summarized above has become increasingly difficult as modern technology has become increasingly
complex. For these reasons the U. S. Patent Office is now
engaged in a research project to apply automatic electronic
devices as means for facilitating the identification of those
previously issued patents that are of pertinent interest to a
newly filed application.

The research effort now under way at the U. S. Patent
Office* will not be reviewed in this section of this book. Nor
will attention be directed to intellectual problems of concept
definition and characterization of subject matter that arise in
establishing compartmentalized classification systems of maximum effectiveness. Rather a mathematical framework will
be provided that can be used as a basis for evaluating how well
a given compartmentalized classification system may serve
the requirements of a given situation. It is believed that such
evaluation will be, in some situations at least, of importance
in making decisions concerning possible applications of given
systems and equipment. Certain systems and equipment may
be used not only to store classified files of documents but also
in conducting filing and arranging operations.

(2) Initial Assumptions

The basic assumptions are the same as throughout this

---

*Bailey, M. F., Lanham, B. E., and Leibowitz, J., "Mech-
anized Searching in the U. S. Patent Office", Journal Patent
Office Society, 35, 566-587, August, 1953.

monograph, namely: (1) that we are confronted by a situation involving a large number--at least several thousand--documents or other graphic records; and (2) that use of the information in the file of documents or records requires that certain of them be selected as being of pertinent interest to a given situation or problem.

It is further assumed that a compartmentalized classification system has been established to meet the requirements stated above. Such a classification system consists, from the intellectual point of view, of a series of headings and subheadings (see, for example, Figure 21) under which individual items are grouped. From the physical point of view, such a classification system may consist of a set of pigeon holes in which individual documents or other records (or copies of the same) have been filed.

To initiate our mathematical analysis we shall assume further: (1) that each item is filed under only one subheading (i. e., in only one pigeonhole); (2) that each search may be satisfied by inspecting the items grouped under a single subheading; (3) that the number of items under a single heading is initially the same for each heading; (4) that this number may be maintained substantially unchanged by reclassifying and establishing new subheadings to provide for additional items entering the file as time passes; and (5) that the establishment of new subheadings can be accomplished without impairment of the second assumption. Our mathematical analysis will consider first, certain consequences of these assumptions in the case of a growing file. Subsequently, we will consider the consequences that arise when an actual situation departs further and further from these assumptions.

(3) Mathematical Analysis

Consider a file containing N_Σ documents or other graphic records in all. In accord with the above mentioned initial assumptions, N_0' will be used to denote the number of items in each of r classes at time t_0. Such a situation might be illustrated by the bar diagram shown in Figure 22.

If incoming items are placed in the various initial r classes, it is to be expected--and experience with actual systems confirms--that the new items will be distributed some-

U. S. Patent Office Classification (Excerpt)

   Class 252

    Subclass

      89 DETERGENTS (FOR USE ON SOLID
           MATERIALS)

      90 - Packages or heterogenous arrangements
      91 -- Impregnated or coated with detergents
      92 -- Separate soap containing and non-soap zones
      93 --- Wrapped or encased soap
      94 - With chemical bleachant, oxidant or reductant
      95 -- Oxidant containing
      96 --- Soap (water soluble fatty-acid or rosin)
           containing
      97 ---- Water-soluble inorganic B, Si or P com-
           pound containing
      98 ---- NH_3, amine, or nitrogen base compound
           containing (except proteins)
      99 -- Water-soluble inorganic B, Si or P com-
           pound containing
     100 --- Acidic
     101 ---- HNO_3 or agua regia containing
     102 --- NH_3, amine or nitrogen base compound
           containing (except proteins)
     103 --- Alkaline

Universal Decimal Classification (Excerpt)

   62.   - Engineering
   621   - Mechanical engineering
   621.1   - Hydraulic power, Hydraulic machines
   621.24 - Hydraulic turbines

Figure 21.
Examples of Classification Headings

CHAPTER IV

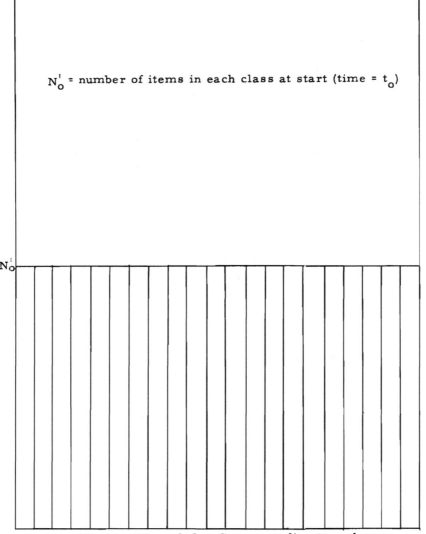

Classification Pigeonholes Corresponding to r classes

Figure 22.

Bar chart at t_o showing equal distribution of items in classification pigeonholes.

what unevenly as shown in Figure 23.   Here and in later equations the following symbols are used:

N = number of items in any one pigeonhole at any time, t.

N' = least number of items in any one pigeonhole at any time, t.

N'_1 = least number of items in any one pigeonhole at a specific time, t_1.

N_r = number of items in the r-th pigeonhole at any time, t.

N_{r_1} = number of items in the r-th pigeonhole at a specific time, t_1.

From Figure 23, it is obvious that at any time, t, the r original classes could be arranged in an order and assigned an order number so that the value of N would increase with the order number.   In other words, N would be smallest for the class of lowest order number, increase with rise in order number and be a maximum for the class of highest order number.   Then N, the number of items in a given class, would be a function of the order number.   This functional relationship will be expected to vary from one situation to another and, for a given situation, significant differences in this functional relationship may be observed at different times.   To illustrate how this functional relationship may be taken into account in evaluating compartmentalized classification systems, we will assume that the value of N for any class increases uniformly with the order number of the classes.   Then for the i-th class among the r classes, at time, t_1.

$$N_{i_1} = N'_1 + k_5 r_i$$

where r_i = order number of the i-th class

k_5 = proportionality constant of $(N_{i_1} - N'_1)$ and r_i

To illustrate these relationships, Figure 24 has been prepared. This might have been drawn as a bar chart showing discrete increments in values of N_i on passing from one class to the next.   It seemed better for illustrative purposes, not to show such increments but to represent the values of N_{i_1} and N_{i_2}, at times t_1 and t_2 as varying continuously with the class order numbers.   Note that, in accord with previously defined symbolism:

N'_2 = least number of items in any one pigeonhole at time, t_2.

N_{r_2} = number of items in the r-th class at time, t_2.

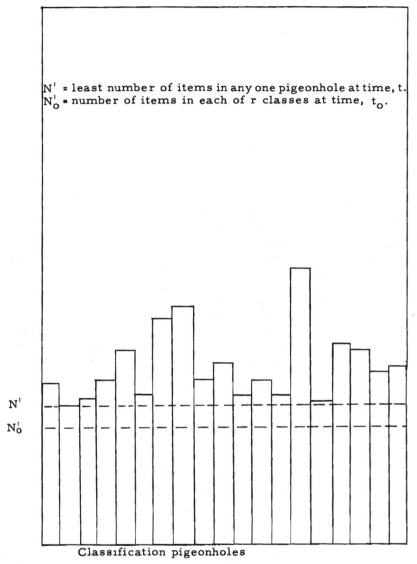

Classification pigeonholes

Figure 23.

Bar chart at time, t_1, showing unequal distribution of items
in classification pigeonholes.

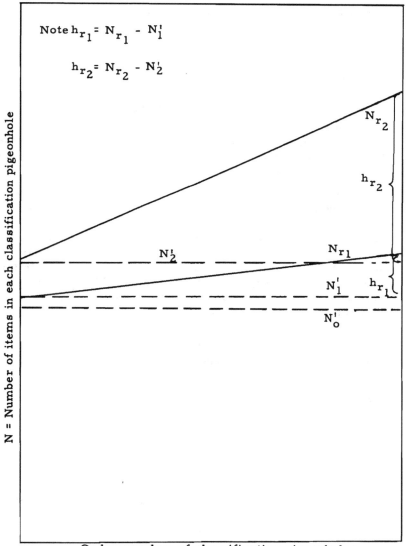

Figure 24.

Relationship between N_o', N' and N_r at successive times t_1 and t_2 (N_1' and N_{r_1} for t_1 and N_2' and N_{r_2} for t_2)

Figure 24 also leads to the definition of a quantity h_r as follows:

$$h_r = N_r - N'$$

Then h_r measures the extent to which the number of items in the r-th class deviates from the minimum number of items in any one pigeonhole at time, t. Figure 25 shows that, as time passes from t_0 to t_1 to t_2, the value of h_r increases. This is an empirical fact based on observations made with actual classification systems. At any time, t, the value of h_r for the r-th class will correspond to some lesser value, h_i, for any one i-th class. At time, t_1, the value of h_i will be denoted by h_{i_1}.

The quantities and relationships, as defined above, are helpful in working out a basis for evaluating the costs of making a search. In line with our initial assumption, we will assume, for the moment, that each search requires personal inspection of the items in a given pigeonhole. It is further assumed that the cost of identifying the correct pigeonhole for a given search is negligible and that the cost of conducting a search is directly proportional to the number of items in the pigeonhole in question. Then for any one search directed to the i-th pigeonhole at any time we may write:

$$S_s = k_3 N_i$$

where S_s = cost of a single search

   k_3 = cost of personal review of a single item

Let S_{sa} = total searching costs per unit time, e.g., a year

   d   = number of searches conducted per unit time, e.g., a year.

To compute S_{sa}, observe that this involves costs due to N' and that these costs do not depend on which class is searched, while costs due to h vary with the class order number r_i. If h is assumed, as before, to be directly proportional to the class order number and if all classes are searched with equal frequency then:

$$S_{sa} = dk_3 \left(N' + \frac{h_r}{2} \right)$$

The assumption that the frequency of search is independent of h_i is unlikely to be in accord with actual experience as

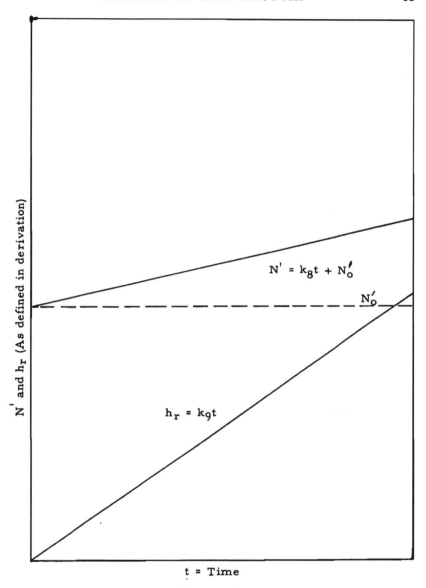

Figure 25.

N' and h_r as functions of Time

(Assuming that the time increments of N' and h_r are independent of time).

the classes with larger values of h correspond to those in
which new documents or records are accumulating more rapidly. More rapid generation of new documents or records is
almost sure to correspond to an area of greater professional
activity with corresponding greater probability of an information request arising in such an area.

Since the classes with higher h values are the more
active areas of interest, the searching costs due to h_i will be
increased by some degree. This may be indicated by C_h,
where $C_h > 1$.

$$S_{sa} = dk_3 \left[N' + C_h \frac{h_r}{2} \right]$$

C_h will doubtless become larger as h_r becomes larger.
In other words, C_h may be expected to be some function of h_r.
For purposes of our discussion and to illustrate how such
functional relationship influences searching costs, we shall
assume direct proportionality.

Then:
$$C_h = k_7 h_r$$
where k_7 is the proportionality constant.

Both N' and h will increase with time, i.e.:

$$N' = f_1(t)$$

$$h_r = f_2(t)$$

In actual cases those two functions, f_1 and f_2, may be different.
If we assume that N' increases by equal amounts in equal time
increments, then:
$$N' = k_8 t + N_0'$$
where k_8 is the increment in N' per unit time.

Similarly, if h (at t_o) = 0 and if h increases by equal
amounts in equal time increments, then

$$h_r = k_9 t$$

where k_9 is the increment in h_r per unit time. See Figure 25
for illustrative graphs.

Substituting for N' and h_r in the equation:

$$S_{sa} = dk_3 \left[N' + C_h \left(\frac{h_r}{2} \right) \right]$$

We have, if $C_h = k_7 h_r$

$$S_{sa} = dk_3 \left[N' + \frac{k_7 h_r^2}{2} \right]$$

And substituting further

$$S_{sa} = dk_3 \left(k_8 t + N_o' + \frac{k_7 k_9^2 t^2}{2} \right)$$

Let ΣS_{sa} = cumulated searching costs at time, t, that is, the sum of all searching costs from time, t_o, to time, t. Then:

$$\frac{d(\Sigma S_{sa})}{dt} = S_{sa}$$

substituting and integrating:

$$\Sigma S_{sa} = dk_3 \left(\frac{k_8 t^2}{2} + N_o' t + \frac{k_7 k_9 t^3}{6} \right)$$

Note that ΣS_{sa} consists of three cost factors:

(1) $dk_3 N_o' t$ due to items in the various classes at $t = 0$.

(2) $\dfrac{dk_3 k_8 t^2}{2}$ due to increase in N' with time. (If $N' - N_o'$ were kept equal to zero, this factor would also equal zero.)

(3) $\dfrac{dk_3 k_7 k_9 t^3}{6}$ due to h. (If h remained equal to zero, this factor would also be equal to zero).

Even if this third category of costs could be eliminated, the second category would cause a continually more rapid rise in searching costs, whether considered on the basis of costs per unit time or total cumulated costs.

Figure 26 presents illustrative graphs for the three cost categories and total cumulated costs.

To counteract the tendency for the second and third cost categories to raise searching costs to intolerable levels, it has been common practice, for example in many patent offices, to reclassify files of documents, especially patents,

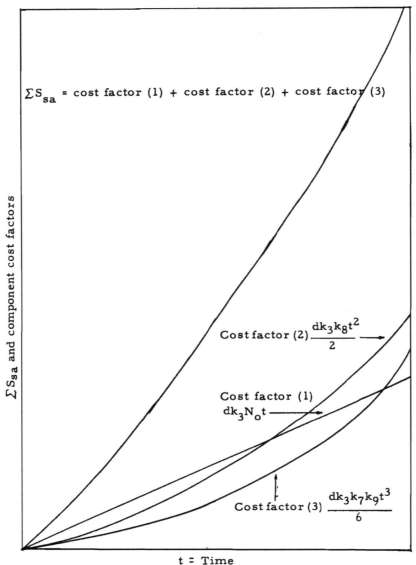

$$\Sigma S_{sa} = \text{cost factor (1) + cost factor (2) + cost factor (3)}$$

Cost factor (2) $\dfrac{dk_3 k_8 t^2}{2}$ $\longrightarrow$

Cost factor (1)
$dk_3 N_o t$ $\longrightarrow$

Cost factor (3) $\dfrac{dk_3 k_7 k_9 t^3}{6}$

t = Time

Figure 26.

ΣS_{sa} and component cost factors as functions
of time.

from time to time. The effect of such reclassification effort on searching costs and the total costs of reclassifying and searching taken together are considered next.

To keep the derivation of equations as simple as possible, consider, first, the following, somewhat idealized case.

N_o' is (as before) same for all r classes.

A is the number of incoming items per unit time and these are equally distributed among the r classes.

N_c is critical value (larger, of course, than N_o) at which reclassification is carried out.

$r + \Delta r$ = number of classes after reclassification.

t_{c1} = time (measured from t_o) at which first reclassification is accomplished.

Then:

A/r = number of items entering each class per unit time

$$(A/r)t_{c1} = N_c - N_o'$$

and:

$$t_{c1} = (N_c - N_o') / (A/r)$$

or:

$$t_{c1} = (\frac{N_c - N_o'}{A}) r$$

The number of classes after the first reclassification, as denoted by r_{c1}, will be:

$$r_{c1} = \frac{N_c r}{N_o'}$$

The cost of the first reclassification will be:

$$C_{r1} = K_r N_c r$$

where

C_{r1} is cost of first reclassification

K_r is cost of reclassifying one item.

Note that the ratio of C_{r1}/t_{c1} is independent of time, except for the rate A of input of items into the systems:

$$\frac{C_{r1}}{t_{c1}} = \frac{K_r N_c r}{(N_c - N_o')(r/A)} = \frac{K_r A N_c}{N_c - N_o'}$$

With continuing inflow of items at rate A, the time for a second reclassification, t_{c2}, will eventually arrive.

$$t_{c2} = \frac{(N_c - N_o') \; r_{c1}}{A}$$

The cost of the second reclassification would be

$$C_{r2} = K_r N_c r_{c1}$$

And

$$\frac{C_{r2}}{t_{c2}} = \frac{K_r N_c r_{c1}}{(N_c - N_o') \; \dfrac{(r_{c1})}{A}} = \frac{K_r N_c A}{N_c - N_o'}$$

Thus the cost of reclassification would increase in direct proportion to the time intervals between classifications, so that the cost of successive reclassification divided by the length of the time interval between them would be a constant, or in terms of equations:

$$\frac{d(\Sigma C_r)}{dt} = \frac{K_r A N_c}{N_c - N_o'}$$

$$\Sigma C_r = (\frac{K_r A N_c}{N_c - N_o'}) \; t$$

where ΣC_r = cumulated cost of reclassification at time, t.

The previous discussion of reclassification has been based on the rather idealized assumption that incoming items are equally distributed among the previously existing classes. It was observed that the time periods between successive reclassifications would lengthen but that there would be a corresponding increase in the number of items requiring attention at each classification.

If we now shift over to an assumption better in accord with observations in actual situations, namely that incoming items are not equally distributed between existing classes (see Figures 23 and 24), then some classes would require reclassification more quickly than others. During unit time, we would expect that the average number of classes requiring reclassification would be:

$$r_c' = \frac{A}{N_c - N_0'}$$

where r_c' = number of classes requiring reclassification per unit time.

The cost for reclassification per unit time would be, as before:

$$\frac{d(\sum C_r)}{dt} = \frac{K_r A N_c}{N_c - N_0'}$$

and the cumulated cost for reclassification at time, t, would also be, as before:

$$\sum C_r = \frac{(K_r A N_c) t}{N_c - N_0'}$$

If each class is promptly reclassified as soon as it contains N_c items then the average value of N' can be kept well below N_c and, depending on circumstances, may be held near N_0'. At the same time h would not assume a large value and in no case would h exceed $N_c - N_0'$. Under such circumstances, searching costs per unit time would be given, with reasonable accuracy, by the equation:

$$\sum S_{sa} = dk_3 (N_0' + N'')$$

where N'' takes care of the average difference between N' and N_0' as the various classes are building up from N_0' to N_c; and:

$$\sum S_{sa} = dk_3 (N_0' + N'')t$$

Figure 27 shows $\sum S_{sa}$, and $\sum C_r$ as well as S_{sa} and $d(\sum C_r)/dt$, based on various previous assumptions, which might be summarized as follows:

(1) Each item is classified into only one pigeonhole.

(2) Each search requires that the contents of only one pigeonhole be inspected.

(3) Each pigeonhole's contents is reclassified as soon as it contains N_c items, so that the number of documents in any class is between N_c and N_0'.

Note that assumption 3 and 1 taken together constitute a fourth assumption.

(4) On reclassification, each item is placed in one pigeonhole, regardless of the increase in number of classes with time.

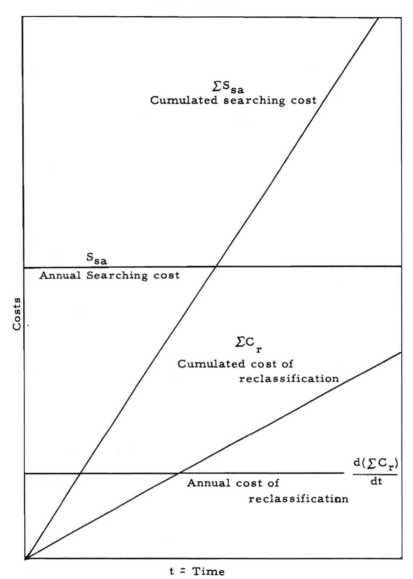

t = Time

Figure 27.

Annual and cumulated costs of searching and reclassifying based on assumptions of page 69.
(Note: At time t = 0 the cumulated costs are both zero)

The fifth assumption remains the same, that is:

(5) The establishment of new subheadings can be accomplished without impairment of the second assumption.

In the history of pigeonhole classifications, assumption 1 is often true at the start when a relatively small number of items permits them to be subdivided into broad mutually exclusive classes with both r (number of classes) and N_0 (number of documents per class) relatively low in value.

With increase in number of classes (r), deviations from assumptions 2 and 4 are observed when working with compartmentalized classification systems.

A deviation from assumptions 2 and 5 arises when accomplishment of a search requires that the contents of more than one pigeonhole shall be inspected. In such a case, the cost of a single search is no longer:

$$S_s = k_3 N_r$$

where S_s = cost of a single search

k_3 = cost of considering a single document

N_r = number of documents in class being searched

Nor will the annual cost of searches be:

$$S_{sa} = dk_3 \left[N' + \frac{C_h h_r}{2} \right]$$

(See page 65)

Instead of d, we will now write $(d + \triangle d')$,

where
$$(d + \triangle d')/d = r_s$$

and:

r_s = average number of classes reviewed per search.

At any time, t, the value of $(d + \triangle d')/d$ may be considered to be an average.

$\triangle d'$ may be regarded as a function of either r or t (i.e. $\triangle d'$ may be regarded as increasing with either r or t).

$$\triangle d' = f(t) = f'(r)$$

Since r increases with t, these two functions would be inter-dependent.

Let us consider $\triangle d'$ as a function of t. In an actual case, this functional relationship may be complex in character. For the sake of simplicity, we shall assume that $\triangle d'$ is directly proportional to t.

Then:

$$\triangle d' = k_{10}t$$

where k_{10} is a proportionality constant

$$S_{sa} = dk_3 \left[N' + \frac{C_h h}{2} r \right]$$

we substitute as before for C_h and N' and also in addition replace d by $d + \triangle d'$, and $\triangle d'$ by $k_{10}t$. We then have:

$$S_{sa} = (d + k_{10}t) k_3 (k_8t + N'_o + \frac{k_7 k_9^2 t^2}{2})$$

In this case, S_{sa} may be considered to consist of two factors:

$$S_{sa} - \text{Factor I and Factor II}$$

where

$$\text{Factor I} = dk_3 (k_8t + N'_o + \frac{k_7 k_9^2 t^2}{2})$$

$$\text{Factor II} = k_{10}t \, k_3 (k_8t + N'_o + \frac{k_7 k_9^2 t^2}{2})$$

For graphical representation, see Figure 28.

Here Factor II is due to the need to search more than one class per search. But as before:

$$\frac{d(\sum S_{sa})}{dt} = S_{sa}$$

As a consequence, $\sum S_{sa}$ will consist of two factors:

$$\sum \text{Factor I} = dk_3 \left[\frac{k_8 t^2}{2} + N'_o t + \frac{k_7 k_9^2 t^3}{6} \right]$$

$$\sum \text{Factor II} = k_{10}k_3 \left[\frac{k_8 t^3}{3} + \frac{N'_o t^2}{2} + \frac{k_7 k_9^2 t^4}{8} \right]$$

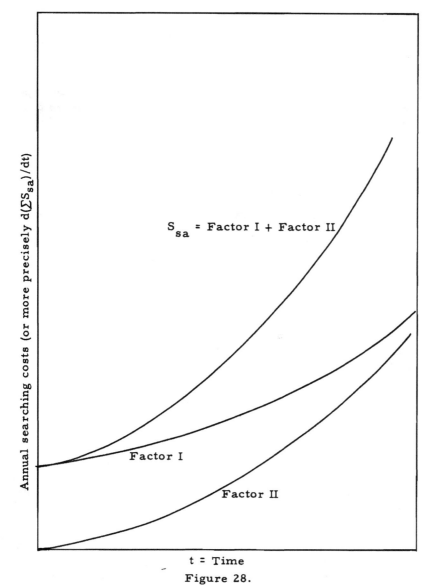

t = Time

Figure 28.

Searching costs as function of time (see pages 72-74).

Graphs of these factors are shown in Figure 29.

These equations for cost factors have been worked out without considering the situation as it would be influenced by reclassification.

By reclassification, we can bring the number of items per pigeonhole to a constant average value, $N_o' + N''$. When d is is independent of t, we then have:

$$S_{sa} = dk_3(N_o' + N'')$$

Replacing d by $dt \triangle d'$ and $\triangle d'$ by $k_{10}t$, we have:

$$S_{sa} = (d + k_{10}t) k_3 (N_o' + N'')$$

Here again, S_{sa} may be considered to consist of two factors:

$$S_{sa} = \text{Factor I} + \text{Factor II}$$

$$\text{Factor I } = dk_3(N_o' + N'')$$

$$\text{Factor II} = k_{10}t k_3 (N_o' + N'')$$

Graphical representation in Figure 30 shows that Factor II increases steadily with time, even though reclassification maintains the number of items in a pigeonhole at a low level, namely between N_c and N_o'.

Similarly cumulative searching costs, $\sum S_{sa}$, may be expressed, in this case also by two factors:

$$\sum \text{Factor I} = dk_3t (N_o' + N'')$$

$$\sum \text{Factor II} = \frac{k_{10}k_3t^2}{2} (N_o' + N'')$$

Figures 30 and 31 illustrate how these cost factors would work out with respect to respective trends.

Deviations from assumption 4 (p. 69) are observed to occur as the classification is made more ramified by increasing the number of classes. Instead of being assigned to only one pigeonhole, there is an increasing tendency for the items on file to be assigned to $1 + p$ pigeonholes.

Here p may be regarded as a function of either r or t, i.e.,

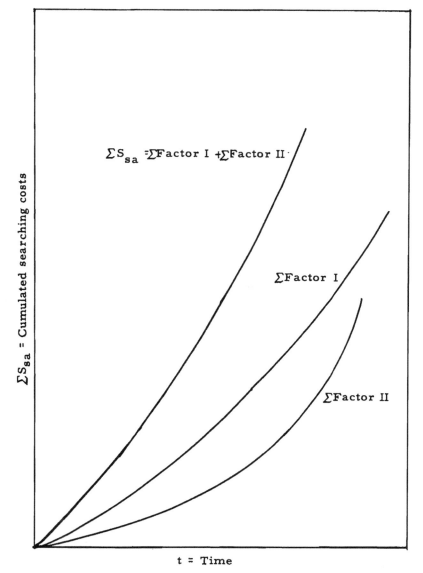

Figure 29.

Cumulated searching costs as function of time

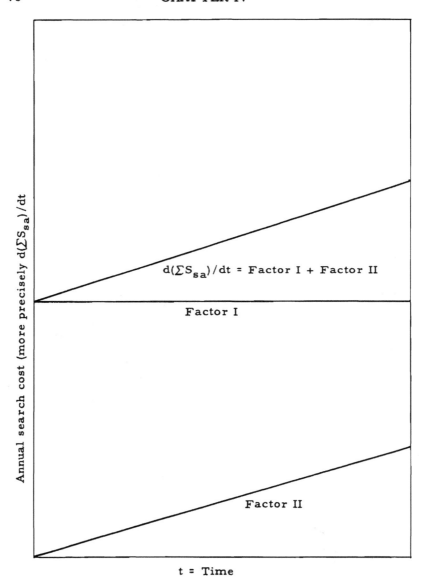

Figure 30.

Searching costs as a function of time

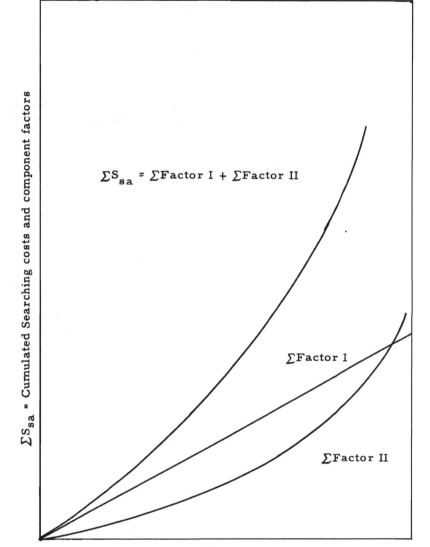

Figure 31.

Cumulated searching costs as a function of time

p may be regarded as increasing with either r or t.

$$p = f(t) = f'(r)$$

Since r increases with t, these two functions will be interdependent.

If we consider p as a function of t, the functional relationship may be complex in character. For the present discussion we shall assume that p is directly proportional to t. Then:

$$p = k_{11}t$$

where k_{11} is a proportionality constant.

As far as generating the need for reclassification is concerned, the effect of p is to increase the effective input of items into the classification system. Where formerly A was the number of input items per unit time, the effective input is now $(1 + p)A$.

Whereas formerly:

$$r'_c = \frac{A}{N_c - N'_o}$$

where r'_c is average number of classes requiring reclassification per unit time.

Now, when A is replaced by $(1 + p)A$, we have:

$$r'_c = \frac{(1 + p)A}{N_c - N'_o}$$

Or, if $p = k_{11}t$ (as we assumed), then:

$$r'_c = \frac{(1 + k_{11}t)A}{N_c - N'_o}$$

By definition of K_r and N_c

$$d(\Sigma C) = K_r N_c r'_c = K_r N_c A \frac{(1 + k_{11}t)}{N_c - N'_o}$$

Integrating:

$$\Sigma C_r = \frac{(K_r A N_c)}{(N_c - N'_o)}t + \frac{(K_r A N_c)}{(N_c - N'_o)} \frac{(k_{11}t^2)}{2}$$

Here again we have two cost factors:

$$\sum \text{Factor 1} = \frac{(K_r A N_c)}{(N_c - N_o')} t$$

$$\sum \text{Factor 2} = \frac{(K_r A N_c)}{(N_c - N_o')} \frac{(k_{11} t^2)}{2}$$

Reclassification cost per unit time also may be regarded as made up of two factors:

$$\text{Factor 1} = \frac{K_r N_c A}{N_c - N_o'}$$

$$\text{Factor 2} = \frac{K_r N_c A k_{11} t}{2 (N_c - N_o')}$$

Figures 32 and 33 show example graphs of these cost factors. Factors 1 and 2 may be regarded as indicating annual costs for reclassifying and the $\sum C_r$ and its factors indicate cumulative reclassifying costs at time t.

Another factor in reclassifying costs arises from the fact that subclasses increase much more rapidly in many classification systems than the main headings or main classes. It is usually impossible in highly ramified classification systems to reclassify individual subclasses independently. Rather a group of subclasses must be reclassified together, and this may involve reclassifying a number of classes whose number of items is below the critical value, N_c. The average N_c, in the classes being reclassified, would thus be effectively lowered with time and would probably tend to approach an asymptotic value between N_o' and N_c as defined on page 67. Let this asymptotic value be N_{ca}. Then this situation may be approximated by considering a time interval during which N_c decreases at a uniform rate to N_{ca} and remains constant thereafter. Figure 34 presents a graph of this situation. From equations on page 78 and above, this lowering in the value of N_c can be expected to increase the cost of reclassifying significantly.

Since:

$$r'_c = \frac{A}{N_c - N_o'}$$

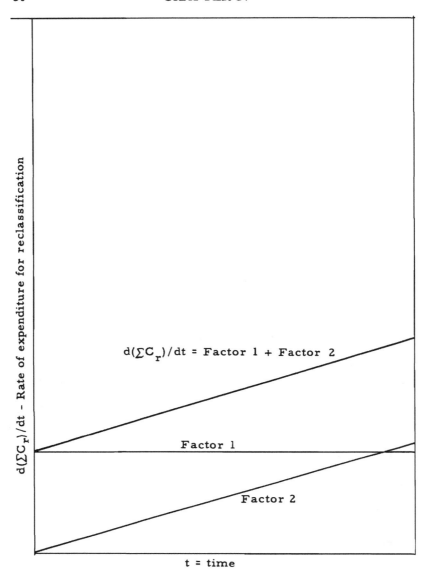

Figure 32.

Rate of expenditure for reclassification as function of
time

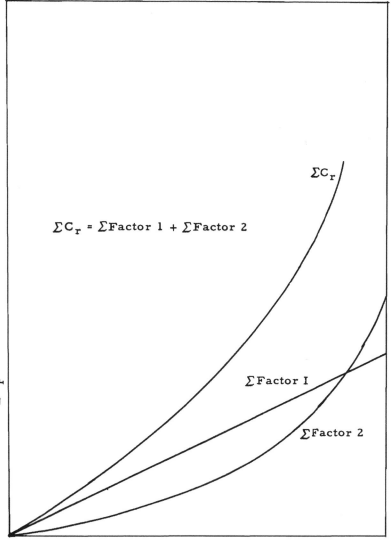

t = Time

Figure 33.

Cumulated reclassification costs as function of time

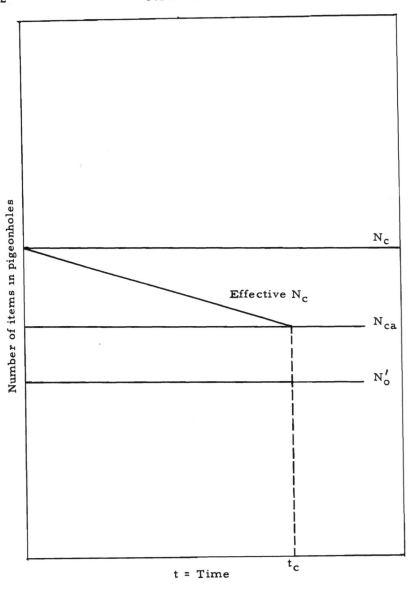

Figure 34.

Change in effective N_c with time

a progressive lowering of the effective value of $N_c - N_o'$ has
the same effect on r_c' as an increase in A. The effect of such
an increase has already been investigated. Hence both increase in number of classes to which an item may be assigned
and also increase in classes that are involved in reclassification that contain less than N_c items will have an additive effect.

It may seem unrealistic on page 72 to write:

$$\triangle d' = k_{10}t$$

as this implies that the number of pigeonholes to be searched
continues to increase as time passes. It must not be forgotten,
however, that the number of classes also increases, as discussed on pages 75 and 78. The same observations could be
made with regard to the factor p as discussed on pages 75 and
78. The point is that continuing increases in r will prevent the
number of classes in the system from imposing ceilings on
either $\triangle d'$ or p.

It should also be noted that $\triangle d'$ and p may be zero during
the early stages of development of a pigeonhole classification
system. Then at some stage, corresponding to a critical stage
of evolution, $\triangle d'$ and p may gradually begin to increase. The
time that this occurs may, of course, be different for $\triangle d'$
and p. Furthermore, the effect of these factors may be slight
at first and consequently may be overlooked or talked down as
of no importance.

Reclassification costs may be regarded, from one point of
view, as annual costs that are incurred to prevent excessive
annual searching costs (See pages 62, 65 and 67). From
another, equally valid, point of view, reclassification costs
might be considered as a tax levied on the system to maintain
its effectiveness. Cumulated reclassification costs constitute
the sum of the continuing tax levied when using pigeonholes as
the mechanical device to facilitate searching operations. If,
by investment in more efficient equipment, reclassification
costs may be eliminated or greatly reduced, important savings
may be effected. If, at the same time, searching costs may
be reduced, a further margin of saving--both in dollars and
manpower--may be effected. (See Figures 35, 36 and 37).

To develop systems for applying equipment more versatile

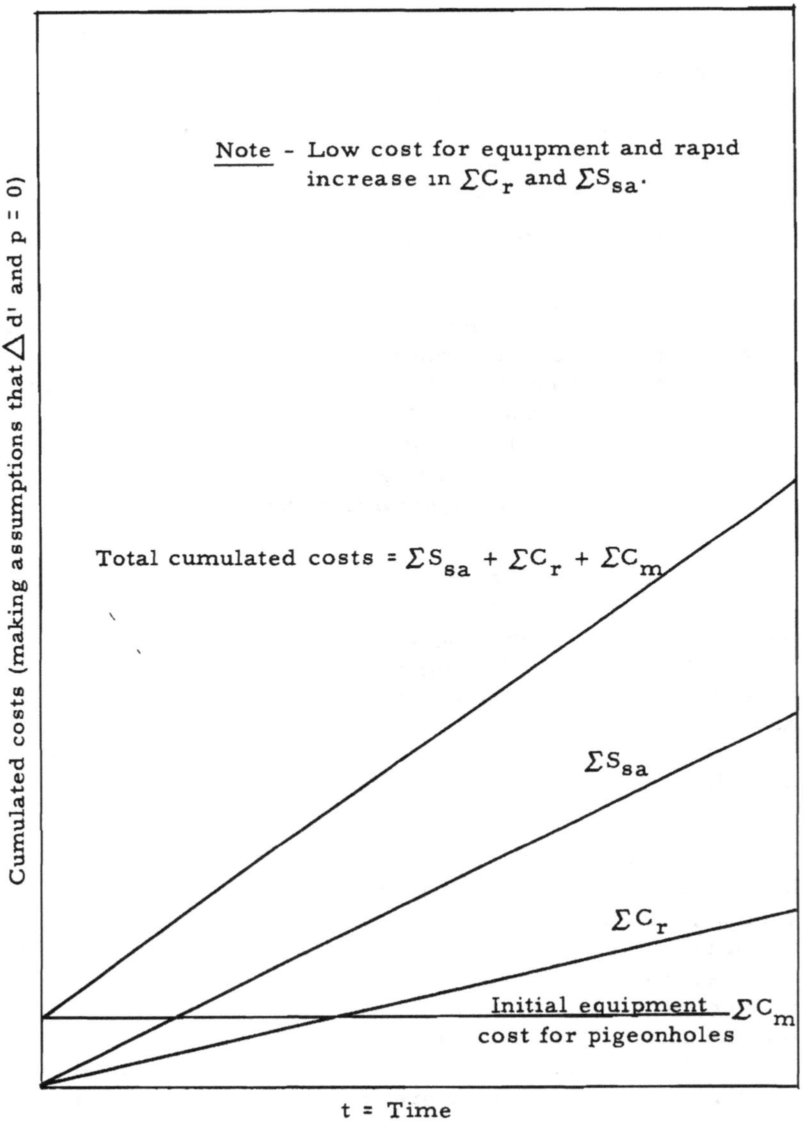

Figure 35.

Cumulated costs as function of time

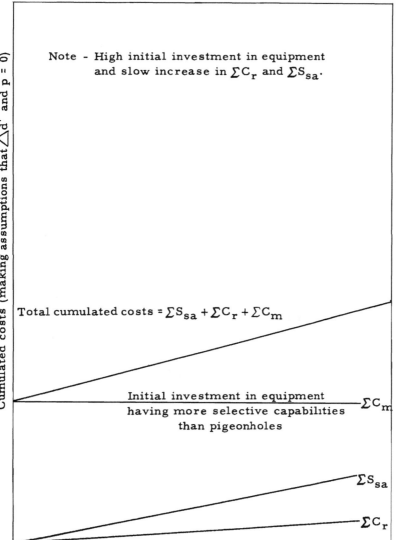

Figure 36.

Cumulated costs as function of time

CHAPTER IV

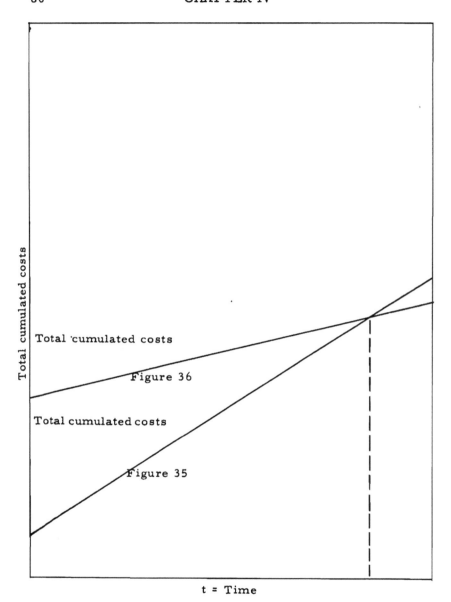

Figure 37.

Comparison of cumulated costs of Figures 35 and 36

than pigeonholes, it is, however, necessary to take into account the role of characteristics as means for identifying items of pertinent interest, as reviewed in Chapter II and III.

D. Alphabetized Indexing

(1) Introductory Notes

Primitively simple mechanical devices--e. g., a set of pigeonholes--may be used as equipment for establishing compartmentalized classification as discussed in Section C of this chapter. This does not mean, however, that more versatile equipment may not be used to establish and maintain such classification consisting of fixed groupings. Whether such application of versatile equipment is advantageous and advisable will depend on purposes to be served and such factors as number of documents, character and complexity of their contents, frequency of use, urgency and related requirements.

Other primitively simple devices may be used to establish and maintain alphabetized indexes, which in essence consist of an ordered array of symbols used to designate the characteristics of various items, especially graphic records of one kind or another. The symbols ordinarily used in constructing indexes are words and phrases that are arrayed in accord with the alphabetical order of the letters. Other symbols, e. g., molecular empirical formulas, and other appropriate ordering rules sometimes provide the basis for generating arrays that are similar to alphabetized indexes and that serve the same general purpose of facilitating the identification of documents of pertinent interest to a given problem or situation.

In constructing indexes, the symbols that are used to characterize various aspects of subject contents of documents may be set up in arrays with the aid of various simple mechanical devices. For example, the indexes of books or periodicals may be written or printed as lists of words or other symbols. Alternately, each unit in the array--or index entry--may be entered on a separate unit record as, for example, in the card catalogs of libraries.

Whether application of given equipment on the basis of alphabetized indexes or similar arrays is advisable in a certain situation will depend, of course, on the various factors that

characterize specific situations. In order to provide a basis
for evaluating such application of systems or equipment in a
given situation, the following analysis of cost factors involved
in using and generating indexes is presented.

(2) Cost Factors in Use of Alphabetized Indexes

As previously noted, alphabetized indexes and similar
arrays are based on an orderly sequence of words or similar
symbols. The rule for ordering the array, e.g., the alphabetical sequence of letters, permits much time and effort to
be conserved in locating any one entry--or a number of
entries--in the array. The various index entries denote, of
course, the characteristics of the subject matter of the items
of information to which the index pertains. In other words, the
index entries provide leads to various documents or similar
records (or to various sections of the same). Actual use of
an index involves both identifying those entries that are effective leads, and then, with their aid, locating documents or
records of possible interest and finally personally inspecting
such items to effect positive identification of pertinent information.

More concisely expressed, the use of indexes may be considered to involve five cost factors* as follows:

I.   Cost of deciding which index entries should be con-
     sulted. (As discussed subsequently, the costs
     involved in this step depend greatly on the nature and
     scope of the information requirement to be serviced).

II. Cost of locating various headings in the ordered
     array. (Both the extent of the array and the number
     of entries to be consulted are of decisive importance).

III. Cost of deciding which headings and subheadings
     appear likely to lead to documents or records of
     sufficient pertinent interest to warrant their personal
     inspection. (Alphabetized indexes and similar arrays
     are often so constructed that various headings are

---

* It should, perhaps, be emphasized again, that costs as outlined here may involve not merely dollar appropriations, but
also costs reckoned in elapsed time or in amount of effort on
the part of expert personnel in short supply.

accompanied by subheadings whose purpose is to facilitate decision as to whether it is worthwhile to review personally the documents or records to which the headings and subheadings refer. When making use of lengthy detailed indexes, considerable costs may be involved in reviewing headings and subheadings and making decisions as to which documents or records are likely to be of sufficient pertinent interest to warrant personal review. These considerations are of importance both in deciding whether to use a given system or equipment in connection with an alphabetized index or similar arrays, and also in establishing indexing policy in conjunction with a given application).

IV. Cost of acquiring the records to which the various selected entries or their subheadings refer. (In an index system based on devices, such as micro cards, that provide a copy of the document in association with the index entries or subheadings, this cost may be much less than would be the case in withdrawing the original documents in conventional form from extensive files or from libraries. On the other hand this cost is likely to be higher when making use of conventional files, in which documents or records are arrayed by acquisition number or similar filing arrangement).

V. Cost of inspecting documents or records to effect positive identification of pertinent items. (Costs incurred under this heading correspond to the costs involved, when using a classification system, in personally inspecting the documents or records grouped in one or more pigeonholes or similar compartments).

Thus, for any one search, using an index, we may break down the cost, S_s, into five component costs:

$$S_s = S_I + S_{II} + S_{III} + S_{IV} + S_V$$

where S_s = cost for a single search,

S_I, S_{II}, S_{III}, S_{IV}, S_V = various cost factors as summarized above.

Attention will next be directed to each of these five cost factors.

Cost Factor, S_I.

The cost in time and effort involved in deciding which index entries should be consulted may vary widely. In simple cases of using alphabetized indexes, this cost factor may be so slight as to be negligible. For example, when using the telephone directory preparatory to making a phone call, no appreciable effort will be involved, as a rule, in deciding what entry to consult. On the other hand, a comprehensive search of a fairly broad subject, e. g. dyes for cellulose acetate rayon, may require a considerable amount of effort in deciding which headings to consult. It is by no means exceptional to be compelled to spend considerable time working with an index to determine what entries are likely to lead to items of pertinent interest. In extreme cases, especially when servicing information requirements whose definition of scope necessarily involves generic concepts predominantly, this cost may be so great as to render detailed indexes of little value in conducting searching operations. This cost factor is influenced predominantly, therefore, by the nature and scope of the information requirement. The background and experience of the person using the index is also of decisive importance in this initial step in using indexes.

It should be emphasized that extensive alphabetized indexes are built up as a rule of large numbers of highly specific headings of narrow scope. Broad headings are used as a rule in such indexes only to refer to review papers or similar reports of general investigations. This is the situation that is encountered, for example, with the well-known subject indexes of Chemical Abstracts.

There can be little doubt, that the magnitude of the cost factor S_I increases with the number of index headings that need to be consulted in order to satisfy an information requirement. This means that--

$$S_I = f(r_s)$$

where r_s = number of index entries that need to be consulted. This functional relationship between S_I and r_s may not be easy to determine in an actual situation but such difficulty cannot be allowed to become an excuse for disregarding the cost factor, S_I . For simplicity in further discussion, we shall assume that S_I increases in direct proportion with r_s, that is to say:

$$S_I = k_{12} r_s$$

where k_{12} is the cost of deciding to consult some one index entry.

We shall return to further consideration of this cost factor in subsequent paragraphs of this section.

Cost Factor, S_{II}.

After the initial step of deciding that certain headings shall be consulted, it becomes necessary to locate them in the alphabetized index or similar array. The cost of locating a single entry in an extensive array certainly increases with the number of headings in the array. Here again, the functional relationship between the cost of locating a single entry and the number of headings in the index array may be different under different circumstances. For simplicity in subsequent discussion, we will assume direct proportionality. In other words, we shall assume that the cost for locating a single entry will be $k_{13} r_i$, where r_i is the total number of entries in an index array and k_{13} is a proportionality constant. For a given search that requires a total of r_s headings to be consulted, we will then have:

$$S_{II} = k_{13} r_s r_i$$

When an index is constructed with the aid of simple devices such as printed lists or ordinary file cards, its consultation and hence the cost factor, S_{II}, involves personal effort exclusively. More complex arrangements may prove advantageous in which the consulting of an index is accomplished automatically with the aid of automatic devices. Discussion of such operations is deferred to Chapter VI. For the present, attention will be centered on costs involved in personal inspection of alphabetized or similarly ordered arrays.

Cost Factor S_{III}

In estimating the costs of examining the various index entries, once they have been located in the array, it must not

be overlooked that, quite frequently, a main index entry will
be accompanied by a number of subheadings. These are
usually provided to facilitate decision as to whether the documents or records to which they refer are likely to be of pertinent interest to a given information requirement. If, on an
average, there are N_s such subheadings under each index
entry, then the number of such subheadings requiring consideration in a search involving r main entries will be $N_s \, r_s$. If
the cost of examining a single subheading is k_{14}, then we have:

$$S_{III} = k_{14} \, N_s \, r_s$$

As previous discussion has suggested, a certain fraction,
denoted by p_1, of the subheadings consulted in any one search
will be decided, at this stage, to give sufficient evidence of
leading to pertinent information to warrant obtaining the documents or records and reviewing them personally. The other
fraction $(1-p_1)$, will be eliminated at this stage as of no further
interest. Accordingly the cost factor, S_{III}, may be considered
to consist of two component factors, namely:

1. Costs of eliminating certain subheadings from further
    consideration:
$$S_{III_1} = (1-p_1) \, k_{14} N_s r_s$$

2. Costs of deciding documents, to which certain sub-
    headings refer, are to be considered further:
$$S_{III_2} = p_1 k_{14} N_s r_s$$

In evaluating possible applications of various systems, these
two cost factors may require separate consideration as is discussed subsequently (pages 114-115).

Cost Factor S_{IV}

The cost of acquiring the individual records to which the
various selected entries or accompanying subheadings refer
may vary considerably depending on circumstances. We shall
assume, for purposes of our discussion, that it is possible to
arrive at an average cost for acquiring a document or record
once it has been identified as of sufficient probable interest to
warrant personal review. This average cost we will denote by
k_{15}. When using a conventional type of file or library, the

average value of k_{15} can be expected to be much higher than when using a recording medium, e. g. hand-sorted punched cards with microfilm inserts, that can accommodate, on a single unit record, both coded information and also graphic material in photographic form.

On an average, each subheading in the index will refer to more than one document and this average number will be denoted by N_d. Then the cost factor under consideration will be given by the equation:

$$S_{IV} = k_{15}N_d p_1 N_s r_s$$

Cost Factor S_V

The cost of personal review of a single document or record to which use of the index has directed attention is, of course, the same as for examining a single document or record to which a classification system has directed attention. This cost has been denoted in an earlier section of this book by k_3. Hence, the cost factor under consideration will be given by the equation:

$$S_V = k_3 N_d p_1 N_s r_s$$

As a result of such review of documents or records to which use of the index directed attention, a certain fraction, denoted by p_2, of these items will be found to be of actual pertinent interest. The remainder, a fraction denoted by $(1 - p_2)$, will be rejected as of no interest. As a consequence, cost factor S_V may be regarded as consisting of two components.

1. Cost of reviewing documents and records of no pertinent interest.

$$S_{V_1} = (1 - p_2)k_3 N_d p_1 N_s r_s$$

2. Cost of reviewing documents and records of pertinent interest

$$S_{V_2} = p_2 k_3 N_d p_1 N_s r_s$$

It must be emphasized that k_3, namely the average cost of personal review of a single document or graphic record, is likely to be high. For this reason, cost factor S_{V_1}, namely the cost of reviewing items of no pertinent interest, is likely to prove particularly important in evaluating the usefulness and efficiency of the retrieving and correlating power of an indexing system.

Resume and Discussion of Analysis of Cost of Using Indexes

For any one search, the cost, denoted by S_s, is broken down into five component costs:

$$S_s = S_I + S_{II} + S_{III} + S_{IV} + S_V$$

S_I, the cost of deciding which index entries to consult, depends on the nature of the information requirement, which may be characterized by the number of index entries that need to be consulted. Hence:

$$S_I = f(r_s)$$

where r_s is the number of index entries that need to be consulted.
As a basis for our discussion, we have assumed:

$$S_I = k_{12}r_s$$

where k_{12} is the average cost of deciding to consult some one entry

S_{II}, the cost of locating the entries in the alphabetized or similar array, increases with the number of index entries, r_i, that make up the array. Assuming for purposes of discussion, direct proportionality, we have

$$S_{II} = k_{13}r_s r_i$$

where k_{13} is the average cost of locating any one entry in an array of r_i entries.

S_{III}, the cost of examining the various index entries and their subheadings is given by the equation:

$$S_{III} = k_{14}N_s r_s$$

where N_s is the average number of subheadings under each entry and k_{14} is the cost of examining a single subheading. (If there are no subheadings in the index, then N_s is equal to unity. In this case, the index entry may be regarded as its own subheading).

Cost factor, S_{III}, may be considered to consist of two components.

1. The cost of eliminating certain subheadings from
    further consideration is given by:

$$S_{III_1} = (1 - P_1)k_{14}N_s r_s$$

where p_1 is the probability that a given subheading is of
interest.

2. The cost of deciding to examine the documents to
    which certain subheadings refer is given by:

$$S_{III_2} = P_1 k_{14} N_s r_s$$

S_{IV}, the cost of acquiring individual documents or records,
is given by:

$$S_{IV} = k_{15} N_d P_1 N_s r_s$$

where k_{15} is the average cost of acquiring a single document
or record from the file, library or similar source. N_d is the
average number of documents referred to by a single subheading.

S_V, the cost of personally reviewing documents to which
the index directs attention, is given by:

$$S_V = k_3 N_d P_1 N_s r_s$$

where k_3* is the average cost of reviewing a single document
or record.

Cost factor, S_V may be considered to consist of two
components.

(1) The cost of personal examination to eliminate certain
     documents or records from further consideration is
     given by:

$$S_{V_1} = (1 - P_2)k_3 N_d P_1 N_s r_s$$

where p_2 is the average probability that any one document
being personally reviewed will prove to be of pertinent interest.

(2) The cost of personal examination to determine that
     certain documents contain information of pertinent
     interest is given by:

---

* See page 34 for first introduction of this constant.

$$S_{V_2} = P_2 k_3 N_d P_1 N_s r_s$$

The various cost factors involved in a single search may be summarized in a single equation:

$$S_s = S_I + S_{II} + S_{III_1} + S_{III_2} + S_{IV} + S_{V_1} + S_{V_2}$$

$$S_s = k_{12} r_s + k_{13} r_s r_i + (1 - P_1) k_{14} N_s r_s + P_1 k_{14} N_s r_s$$
$$+ k_{15} N_d P_1 N_s r_s + (1 - P_2) k_3 N_d P_1 N_s r_s + P_2 k_3 N_d P_1 N_s r_s$$

Cumulative Costs of Using Indexes

The preceding analysis of cost factors involved in the use of alphabetized indexes has been based on the consideration of a single search. Our analysis shows that r_s, the number of index entries that must be consulted in carrying out a search, plays a particularly important role in determining costs. As the final equation for S_s indicates, each of the cost factors S_I, S_{II}, S_{III}, S_{IV} and S_V tends to go up as r_s increases.

In some situations, e.g., in using the telephone directory preparatory to making phone calls, the average value of r_s remains during the course of a year at a low value either equal to or only slightly greater than unity. In such situations, when only one, or at most a very few index entries, need be consulted for each search, the correspondingly low average value of r_s makes it possible to express the annual cost of using an index by the equation:

$$S_{sa} = (k_{12} r_s + k_{13} r_s r_i + k_{14} N_s r_s + k_{15} N_d N_s r_s + k_3 N_d N_s r_s) A_s$$

where S_{sa} is the annual cost of using the index. A_s is the number of searches conducted annually.

The p_1 factor in the general equation has been put equal to unity in this simplified equation. This is equivalent to assuming that the low average value of r_s corresponds to the need to inspect personally all the documents to which reference is made by the single entry (or very small number of entries) consulted for each search. If this were not true then the index would be failing its purpose at least partially and this fact could be expressed by attaching a suitable coefficient to A_s, to indicate that fraction of the searches in which consultation of one or a few index entries sufficed for an unsuccessful termination of the search. For such searches the annual costs may be expressed by:

$$S_{sa_I} = (k_{12}r_s + k_{13}r_s r_i + k_{14}N_s r_s)uA_s$$

where u = fraction of searches terminated on considering one or a few index entries.

The cost of searches involving personal review of the documents would then be:

$$S_{sa_{II}} = (k_{12}r_s + k_{13}r_s r_i + k_{14}N_s r_s + k_{15}N_d N_s r_s + k_3 N_d N_s r_s)(1-u)A_s$$

Total annual costs would be the sum of S_{sa_I} and $S_{sa_{II}}$ as given by these two equations.

Information requirements are not necessarily limited, however, in all circumstances to searches that involve consulting only one or at most a very few index entries. In the more general case, the information requirements will be such that accomplishment of the corresponding searches will make it necessary to consult widely different numbers of entries for various searches. This general case may be illustrated by Figure 38 which is based on a sufficiently large number of searches to provide a significant sample. Figure 38 is constructed by proceeding as follows: (1) The individual searches are arranged in the order of ascending number of index entries that had to be consulted. (2) Each search is then assigned an order number so that the searches involving a lesser number of index entries receive the lower order numbers. If two or more searches involve the same number of index entries, they do not receive the same order number but arbitrarily assigned successive order numbers. In this way, it becomes possible to indicate by a single point on the graph both the order number, s_n, of a search and the number, r_s, of index entries that the search involved. These points then may be represented, to a very close approximation, by a continuous curve. An example of such a curve is shown in Figure 38.

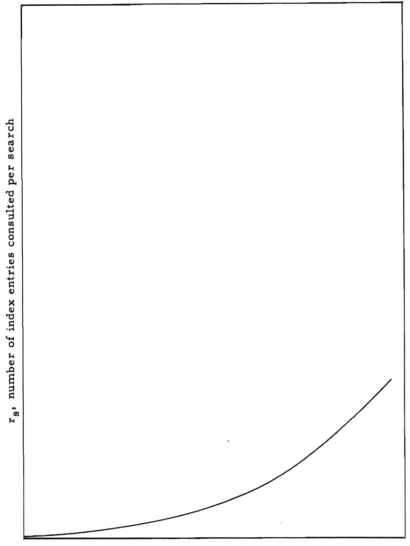

n_s . Order number of searches

Figure 38.

Number of entries consulted per search as function of
order number of search

It is perhaps immediately obvious that the shape of the curve exemplified by Figure 38 will be strongly influenced by the nature of the information requirements to be serviced. Thus, for a given index, we may have situations in which all but a very few searches are satisfied by consulting either one or a very few index entries. The curve for such a case may be exemplified by curve 1 in Figure 39. Additional curves depicting other functional relationships between r_s and s_n are also shown in Figure 39.

Enough has been said to establish the point that the functional relationship between r_s and s_n may vary greatly in character. Thus, as an example of the general relationship:

$$r_s = f(s_n)$$

we might have the simple case of direct proportionality:

$$r_s = k_{16} s_n$$

where k_{16} is the proportionality constant.

It appears doubtful, in the light of experience in constructing and using indexes that this direct proportionality relationship will be encountered at all frequently in actual practice.

A more probable type of functional relationship between r_s and s_n is given by the power series:

$$r_s = a' + b' s_n + c' s_n^2 + d' s_n^3 \; - \; - \; - \; - \; -$$

where a', b', c', d' are constants that characterize such curves as curve 2 in Figure 39.

If curve 2 in Figure 39 or similar curves are based on the searches for some one year, then searching costs for the year may be worked out by proceeding along the following lines: We first note that the cost for any one search, in accord with previous analysis, is given by:

$$S_s = k_{12} r_s + k_{13} r_s r_i + k_{14} N_s r_s + k_{15} N_d P_1 N_s r_s + k_3 N_d P_1 N_s r_s$$

which may be rewritten as

$$S_s = \left[k_{12} + k_{13} r_i + k_{14} N_s + (k_{15} + k_3) N_d P_1 N_s \right] r_s$$

Here S_s is the cost of any one search for which r_s and s_n will

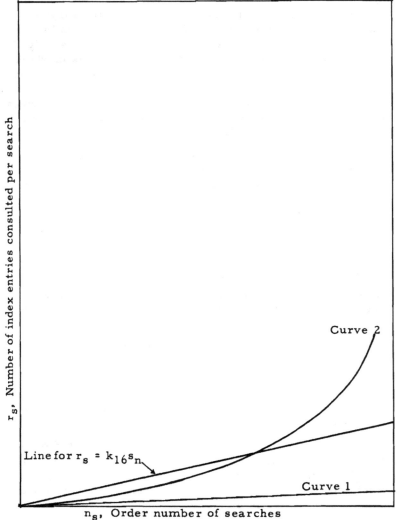

Figure 39.

Curves showing number of entries consulted per
search as function of order number for different
groups of searches

have certain values. Since the total annual searching costs, S_{sa}, are the sum of the costs for individual searches, we may write:

$$\frac{dS_{sa}}{ds_n} = S_s$$

If now the various factors, such as k_{12}, N_s, p_1 etc. within the square brackets

$$\left[k_{12} + k_{13}r_i + k_{14}N_s + (k_{15} + k_3)N_d p_1 N_s\right]$$

are either all constant or the value of the square bracket remains substantially constant with respect to changes in s_n, we may then write, in general:

$$\frac{dS_{sa}}{ds_n} = S_s = Kr_s = Kf(s_n)$$

and

$$S_{sa} = \int Kf(s_n)ds_n$$

or, specifically, when r_s may be expressed as a power series of s_n:

$$\frac{dS_{sa}}{ds_n} = K(a' + b's_n + c's_n^2 + d's_n^3 -----)ds_n$$

and

$$S_{sa} = \int K(a' + b's_n + c's_n^2 + d's_n^3 -----)ds_n$$

In applying these equations to evaluating the annual costs of using an index it is necessary to take the following into account:

(1) It should not be assumed without confirmation that K is independent of s_n. To shed light on this point analysis of the various factors that determine K should be conducted for searches of widely different s_n values.

(2) If K varies with s_n, a simple functional relationship may be developed, thus permitting more accurate evaluation of annual costs of index searching than would be possible otherwise.

Our discussion, up to this point, concerning costs involved in using indexes has assumed that, for a given search or group of searches, the index to be used remains unchanged. In certain situations this may indeed be the case. For any

given edition of a large reference word, such as the Encyclo-
pedia Britannica, the index undergoes no change as time
passes.

   With many indexes, however, various kinds of changes
may occur. For example, the card catalog of a library that is
kept up-to-date in its field can scarcely remain static. At the
least, newly acquired books and documents will be cataloged
under old headings as well as under new main subject headings
that may also have to be established to provide leads to information particularly in new fields of research. In terms of our
analysis, there may be a tendency for increase in one or more
of the following factors:

   r_i, total number of main headings.

   N_s, average number of subheadings under a main heading.

   N_d, average number of documents referred to under a
        subheading.

Which of these factors will increase and at what rate will be
determined not only by the amount and kind of new information
but also the policies involved in maintaining the index. In the
case of library card catalogs, increases in r_i and N_s are likely
to occur more slowly than increases in N_d. The costs in time
and effort required to make changes in an extensive set of
subject headings discourage extensive revisions in such indexes. New books and documents are entered under old headings. Thus N_d tends to increase while r_i and N_s may increase
more slowly than might be expected.

   The situation is quite different for an abstract periodical
such as Chemical Abstracts. Here the index user is confronted by a series of previously issued indexes, both annual
and decennial, and a new annual index is issued each year. The
effect on searching costs of a new annual index may be considered by reference to our previous analysis.

   S_I, the cost of deciding which index entries to consult will
increase only slightly, and may not increase at all. A slight
increase may result from introduction of new main headings
and subheadings as a consequence of the development of new
concepts and innovations.

S_{II}, the cost of locating the entries in the new index will be increased by an amount ΔS_{II}. Making the same assumptions as before concerning the relationship between S_{II} and the number of headings in an index array, we would have the equation $\Delta S_{II} = k_{13} r_s \Delta r_i$ where Δr_i is the number of index entries in the annual index.

S_{III}, the cost of examining the various index entries and their subheadings would be increased by a factor $\Delta S_{III} = k_{14} \Delta r_s N_s$ where Δr_s is the number of entries among r_s found in the new annual index.

The increase in S_{IV}, the cost of acquiring documents that appear worthy of personal review would be

$$\Delta S_{IV} = k_{15} N_d p_1 N_s \Delta r_s.$$

Similarly the increase in S_V, the cost of personal review of documents would be $\Delta S_V = k_3 N_d p_1 N_s \Delta r_s.$

As is perhaps obvious, it is assumed here that the values for such factors as N_d, N_s, p_1 and for the proportionality factors are the same for the new annual index as for previously issued indexes. Such assumptions are probably close to the truth insofar as relationships between annual indexes are involved. On the other hand, the values of N_d and N_s are usually considerably larger for the decennial indexes of Chemical Abstracts than for the annual indexes. As a consequence, these factors must be separately evaluated in analyzing the searching costs of the annual and the decennial indexes.

This discussion of the effect of expansion of indexes on the cost of using them has been included to illustrate how their previous analysis provides a basis for forecasting future cost trends. This is particularly important when establishing a new information facility or greatly expanding an old one. Experience shows that there is considerable danger of overlooking one or more important cost factors. With the application of various newer systems or equipment, there is danger not only of neglecting sources of costs but also of overlooking possibilities of achieving savings and other advantages.

Our analysis of the costs of using indexes would be incomplete if attention were not directed to some of the consequences of the high costs (in time, effort and money) that result when the r_s, (the number of entries that must be consulted for a given search) becomes large. The most important of these consequences is that there is a strong tendency not to carry through such searches. Avoidance of such searches by index users sometimes misleads professional indexers and editors of abstract periodicals to argue that such searches are of little or no importance. In terms of practical operations, avoidance of the more time consuming and expensive searches must be equated to a partial failure to exploit available information. Such searches, which draw together information indexed under a large number of entries, are directed as a rule to the retrieval and correlation of widely scattered information.

With the development of specialized electronic searching equipment, new possibilities in this connection are opened up. With newer systems and equipment we could surmount the limitations of indexing systems that operate solely on a fixed array of symbols, as typified by an alphabetized index. As previous discussion has emphasized, the attempt to designate each significant detail of the subject matter of documents by a separate entry in a fixed array leads to a situation in which correlative searches become so tedious and expensive as to impede the efficient use of recorded information. With newer systems and equipment, it becomes possible to characterize the subject contents of graphic records on the basis of broad subject headings. These headings may be used not only as a basis for conducting automatically performed correlative searches but to achieve file subdivision so that a majority of searches will need to be directed to only one or a very few of the subdivisions. One such system for encoding the subject contents of scientific and technical papers has recently been described* and is now being applied on a pilot plant scale in the field of metallurgy. **

---

*   Perry, James W., Kent, Allen and Berry, Madeline M. "Machine Literature Searching", Interscience Publishers, New York, 1956.

** Kent, Allen, Perry, James W. and Booth, Robert E., "Automation in Literature Research--A Report on the ASM Mechanized Literature Searching Project", Metal Progress, Vol. 71, No. 2, 71-75, February, 1957.

(3) Cost of Constructing and Maintaining Indexes and Files

When alphabetized indexes or similar arrays are used as
an aid to locating information of pertinent interest, it is usual
practice to maintain two separate units, one of which is the
index and the other a file of documents or records usually
arranged in a different way than the index. Consideration of
a situation of this type not only permits us to identify various
cost factors, but also provides a basis for estimating the
possible advantages of applying given systems and equipment.
Unusual equipment capabilities, for most advantageous ex-
ploitation, may lead to development and adoption of indexing
procedures rather different from those employed when constructing indexes in the traditional ways, as exemplified by
book indexes or library card catalogs.

To provide a basis for evaluating and planning equipment
applications, the cost of constructing and maintaining conventional indexes and files are analyzed along the following lines:
A. Indexing costs.
    I.   Cost of reviewing and understanding a document
         preparatory to indexing.
    II. Cost of deciding upon appropriate index entries.
    III. Cost of processing index entries preparatory to
         constructing the ordered array of index entries.
    IV. Cost of establishing the ordered array.
B. File Maintainance costs.
    I.   Cost of acquiring or producing one (or more)
         copies of the documents preparatory to establish-
         ing the file.
    II. Cost of processing the documents (in single or
         multiple copies) preparatory to filing.
    III. Cost of conducting the filing operation.
    IV. Cost of providing storage.

The costs involved in indexing and filing operations will
depend in part on circumstances as they exist, especially the
number of documents to be indexed, their format, and their
subject contents, and in part on policy decisions as to indexing
and filing procedures. In order that possibilities opened up by
newer equipment may be worked out to provide maximum advantages in a practical situation, careful analysis of the prin-
cipal factors that control and influence indexing and filing costs

appears advisable. Providing a basis for the analysis of such costs is the purpose of the discussion that follows. Attention will be directed first to the four above-mentioned indexing costs which will be denoted by I_{I_a}, I_{II_a}, I_{III_a}, and I_{IV_a} where the subscript letter, a, indicates that costs are being considered on an annual basis.

Cost Factor I_I.

The cost of reviewing and understanding a document preparatory to indexing will depend on the scope and complexity of its subject contents and also, though usually to a lesser extent, on its format, For a number of documents or records reasonably similar as to subject matter and format, the cost of reviewing and understanding a single document may be formulated as an average value. Then for cost factor I_I, we would write

$$I_{I_a} = k_{17}a$$

where k_{17} is the average cost of reviewing and understanding a single document or other record, and a is the number of documents to be reviewed and indexed annually.

The value of k_{17} will be influenced, to some extent at least, by the indexing policy and this is a point to which we will return subsequently. It should also be noted that k_{17}, the cost of understanding a document preparatory to indexing, classifying or coding is, on an average, greater than k_3, the cost of personally inspecting a document to confirm (or to deny) its pertinence to a given search.

Cost Factor I_{II_a}

The cost of deciding upon appropriate index entries will be strongly influenced by indexing policies, especially the extent to which the indexing is made detailed in character. For documents of a similar scope, subject content, and format, the cost of establishing a single index entry may be formulated as an average value and for cost factor I_{II_a} we may write:

$$I_{II_a} = k_{18}r_d a$$

where k_{18} is the average cost of establishing a single index entry, r_d is the average number of index entries per document and, a is the number of documents to be reviewed and indexed annually.

A shift in indexing policy that results in a considerable change in r_d may influence both k_{18}, the average cost of establishing a single index entry, and also k_{17}, the average cost of reviewing a document or record preparatory to establishing index entries. Rather paradoxically, an indexing policy that imposes a rigid ceiling on the number of entries per document may result in a higher value for k_{18}, as such a policy may result in considerable time and effort being devoted to setting up the limited number of index entries so that they will be most effective. On the other hand, a policy of detailed indexing that results in a higher value of r_d can be expected to require more detailed review of the subject contents of documents with a corresponding tendency for k_{17} to increase.

Cost Factor I_{III_a}

The processing of index entries preparatory to establishing the ordered array usually consists of a number of routine steps, such as transcribing entries either in hand-written or dictated form, and proof-reading, as well as reconciling entries with standard subject heading lists. For purposes of subsequent discussion we will distinguish between routine tasks of a clerical nature, on the one hand, and the reviewing and reconciling of index entries as to consistency, on the other hand. Accordingly we will formulate cost factor I_{III_a} as follows:

$$I_{III_a} = (k_{19} + k_{20})r_d a$$

where k_{19} is the average cost for clerical operations for a single index entry, k_{20} is the average cost for reviewing and reconciling a single index entry, and r_d and a have the same significance as previously.

It is scarcely possible, of course, to compile an index without incurring costs for the clerical routine operations corresponding to k_{18}. On the other hand, an index may be constructed without reviewing and reconciling index entries as to consistency. A sloppily constructed index is an unreliable instrument

that is difficult to use, and consistency among index entries
may be regarded as the key to reliability in the practical use
of an index.   This does not mean, of course, that unlimited
expense in reviewing and reconciling index entries can be
justified.   It is in this connection that skill and judgement on
the part of indexers is particularly valuable.

Cost Factor I_{IV_a}

The cost of establishing the ordered array of index entries
may be formulated in terms of average cost for processing a
single index entry.   Then for cost factor I_{IV_a} we will write:

$$I_{IV_a} = k_{21} ar_d$$

where k_{21} is the average cost of processing a single index
entry and r_d and a have the same significance as before.

The value of ar_d cannot be equated with r_i, the total number of entries in the final array, as a single entry in the final
array may refer to more than one document.   Note, however,
that an increase in r_d as a result of more detailed indexing can
be expected to result in each entry in the final array referring
to a smaller number of documents.   In other words, with more
detailed indexing we may expect the value of r_i to approach ar_d
more closely.   It should also be noted that when the values
of ar_d or r_i are sufficiently high, the costs of establishing
ordered arrays of index entries may be reduced by the introduction of mass production methods.   Such economies may
also be achieved, somewhat as a by-product, when automatic
equipment is introduced primarily to achieve economies in
other directions, e. g., storage.

We shall next direct attention to the various cost factors
involved in establishing and maintaining files.   We shall denote
these cost factors as F_I, F_{II}, F_{III}, and F_{IV}.

Cost Factor F_I

We shall consider this cost factor to consist of (1) the
average acquisition cost F_{I_1} for a single document or record
and (2) the average cost F_{I_2} of obtaining or producing one or

more additional copies for filing purposes.

The cost of acquisition of a document or record from an outside source is not subject to influence by policy decisions regarding indexing, in particular, or other systems for making information available, in general. (The decision to acquire or not to acquire a document or record may be influenced by the design of the information system, but that is a different matter).

The ability at low cost to produce, to file and to store multiple copies of documents or records may influence indexing policy profoundly, as will be discussed subsequently. For the moment, however, we will limit ourselves to formulating F_{I_a} (the annual F_I costs) as follows:

$$F_{I_a} = aF_{I_1} + aF_{I_2}$$

$$F_{I_a} = k_{22}a + k_{23}N_f a$$

where k_{22} is the average cost of acquiring a single document, k_{23} is the average cost of producing a copy of a document for filing purposes, N_f is the average number copies of each document required for filing purposes, a is the number of documents acquired annually.

Cost Factor F_{II}

Costs in processing documents in single or multiple copies preparatory to filing arise as the result of (1) the intellectual analysis of subject contents and (2) the physical handling of the documents.

Costs incidental to the analysis of subject contents have been accorded attention elsewhere in this monograph, especially in the discussions devoted to pigeon-hole classification and costs of indexing. Also, consideration is directed to the costs of subject content analysis in chapter VI.

For the present, attention is focused on those document-processing operations (aside from intellectual analysis) that are necessary in order that filing may be performed.

Filing implies, by its very nature, an arraying of documents in accord with some rule or rules. Such arraying in

turn requires that the documents be marked in some appropriate fashion as a preliminary to filing. In the simplest case,
the documents as received already bear appropriate marking
for filing. An example of this situation is encountered when
maintaining a numerical file of U. S. patents. In this case, the
serial number printed on the patent provides the needed marking for filing and as a consequence, in such a situation, the
cost of processing the documents preparatory to filing may be
virtually non-existent.

The costs denoted by F_{II} may not amount to much when a
single marking is required for each document to be filed. On
an annual basis, such costs might then be expressed by the
equation:

$$F_{II_a} = k_{24}a$$

where k_{24} is the cost of processing a single document during
this step preparatory to filing.
If, on an average for each document, N_f copies are to be
processed preparatory to filing, then this equation would
become:

$$F_{II_a} = k_{24}aN_f$$

If the production of the N_f copies is conducted separately from
their further processing, especially marking preparatory to
filing, it may be necessary to establish office routines involving several distinct steps and the F_{II} costs may thus become
well worthy of consideration. Such costs constitute one possibility for achieving advantage by applying automatic equipment
in which it would be possible to prepare multiple copies of
individual documents and at the same time provide for sorting
on different index entries for the different copies.

Cost Factor F_{III}

The process of filing previously processed documents may
consist essentially of a single operation, namely, inserting a
single copy of each document under some one file heading. In
this simple case, we would expect the filing costs to tend to
increase with the complexity of the filing system, that is, with
the number of headings under which documents are to be filed.
If we denote the number of such headings by r_f, then the cost

of filing a single document will be a function of the number of headings:

$$F_{III} = f(r_f)$$

This functional relationship may vary considerably depending on circumstances and may not be easy or simple to determine. For purposes of subsequent discussion we will assume a simple relationship of direct proportionality. This assumption may be expressed by the equation:

$$F_{III} = k_{25} r_f$$

where k_{25} is the proportionality constant.

If, as before, only one copy of each document is to be inserted in the file and if, furthermore, the number of documents to be filed per year is denoted by a, then annual filing costs would be:

$$F_{III_a} = k_{25} r_f a$$

If the average number of copies of each document being placed in the file is denoted by N_f, then the annual filing costs would be

$$F_{III_a} = k_{25} r_f a N_f$$

In arriving at this equation, we have assumed that the documents--or copies of documents--after marking for filing are not subject to any sorting or arranging operations before placing them in the file. The costs of this simple filing procedure may sometimes be reduced, especially when filing larger batches of documents, by submitting them to a preliminary sorting operation to arrange them in the order that corresponds to the order of the headings of the file. The subsequent filing step is then essentially a collating operation. The equations for the costs under consideration must then be altered to take into account the two-step operation. The cost of preliminary sorting of the documents to be filed, which incidentally is an operation similar to establishing an ordered array of index entries, may be expressed by:

$$F_{III_{1_a}} = k_{26} a N_f$$

where k_{26} is the average cost of sorting and arranging in filing order a single document or a single copy of a document for which multiple copies are being provided.

The costs of the subsequent filing operation, which, as noted, would be essentially a collating operation, would be dependent on the number of headings in the files and also on the number of documents or copies of documents to be filed. If, as before, we assume direct proportionality both with the number of file headings and the number of items to be filed, then the annual filing costs under consideration may be expressed by the formula:

$$F_{III_{2_a}} = k_{27}r_f aN_f$$

where k_{27} is the proportionality constant of the cost of filing a single document to the number of file headings. a and N_f have the same significance as before.

Annual filing costs would then be given by the formulas:

$$F_{III_a} = F_{III_{1_a}} + F_{III_{2_a}}$$

$$F_{III_a} = k_{26}a + k_{27}r_f aN_f$$

The operations and costs incurred on incorporating documents into a file have been discussed in considerable detail as the capabilities of the appropriately designed automatic equipment appear particularly favorable to expediting operations and reducing costs in time, effort and money. This point is discussed further in the subsequent summary discussion on filing costs.

Cost Factor F_{IV}

The costs of providing storage often achieve such decisive importance in maintaining extensive files that a separate section of this chapter has been devoted to their analysis and evaluation. Application of versatile automatic equipment can effect important reductions in annual costs incurred for file storage. The savings so achieved, when considered on a cumulative basis, may be found to provide ample justification for employing automatic equipment in many situations to which

advantageous application might not appear immediately
obvious.

Resume and Discussion of Analysis of File Costs

Annual file costs, denoted by F_a, have been broken down
into four component costs:

$$F_a = F_{I_a} + F_{II_a} + F_{III_a} + F_{IV_a}$$

F_{I_a}, the cost of providing material for filing is broken
down further into $F_{I_{1_a}}$, the cost of acquiring a document or
record from an outside source and $F_{I_{2_a}}$ the cost of producing
one or more copies for filing. Hence:

$$F_{I_a} = F_{I_{1_a}} + F_{I_{2_a}} = k_{22}a + k_{23}N_f a$$

where k_{22} is the average cost of acquiring a single document,
k_{23} is the average cost of producing a copy of a document for
filing purposes, a is the number of documents acquired per
year, N_f is the average number of copies prepared for each
document.

F_{II_a}, the annual cost of preparatory processing, exclusive
of intellectual analysis of subject content, is given by

$$F_{II_a} = k_{24}aN_f$$

where k_{24} is the cost of processing a single copy of a document.

F_{III}, the cost of incorporating documents into a file tends
to increase with the number of file headings. Assuming direct
proportionality:

$$F_{III_a} = k_{25}r_f aN_f$$

where r_f is the number of file headings, k_{25} is the proportionality constant expressing the cost of filing one document or
copy of a document.

Depending on filing procedures, this cost may be broken
down into F_{III_1} the cost of arranging documents into file order
and F_{III_2} the cost of collating them into the file. These costs,

on an annual basis may be given by:

$$F_{III_a} = F_{III_{1_a}} + F_{III_{2_a}} = k_{26} a N_f + k_{27} r_f a N_f$$

where k_{26} is the average cost of arranging one document (or a copy of a document) in file order, k_{27} is the average cost of collating one document (or a copy of a document) into a file.

F_{IV_a}, the annual costs for storing files, were reviewed in a previous section of this chapter.

Indexing Policies

Our analysis of the use and construction of indexes has mentioned a number of variables, in particular:

r_d the average number of index entries per document

r_i the total number of main entries

N_s the average number of subheadings under each main entry

N_d the average number of documents referred to under each subheading.

As our analysis has shown, the values that these variables have in a given set of circumstances are of decisive importance in influencing costs both of constructing and using indexes. It must not be overlooked that decisions as to indexing policies determine the values assumed by these variables in a given situation. For example, if a larger number of more highly specific subjects are chosen as main index entries, then r_i will be greater than would be the case if a smaller number of generic subjects were chosen. If the product $r_i N_s$ remains constant or nearly so for different indexing policies, then the value of N_d (the average number of documents referred to under each subheading) can be expected to remain reasonably constant unless there is a large change in the degree of detail taken into account in indexing. Experience has shown that indexes constructed with broader or more generic, main headings are better adapted for correlating scattered information while indexes constructed with the more specific type of main headings are more efficient as tools for locating individual facts and specific data. The prewar indexes of <u>Chemisches</u>

<u>Zentralblatt</u> and of <u>Chemical Abstracts</u> may be cited as
examples in this connection. Both types of indexes, regardless of policy decisions, are almost completely ineffective in
facilitating searches whose scope is defined in terms of combinations of generic concepts. More precisely, such indexes
fail to facilitate such searches except in those rare instances
in which a combination of generic concepts is found either as
a main entry or as a combination of a main entry and a subheading.

Appropriately designed automatic equipment opens a wide
range of possibilities in conducting subject indexing. Costs of
preparing various arrays appear likely to be low enough that
it may prove advantageous to construct duplicate indexes, with
one index based on a smaller number of generic headings to
facilitate broad correlations, and with another index based on
more specific headings to facilitate drawing together fragmen-
tary information. The possibilities of searching and retrieving
that would thus be provided by grouping of items under headings would be supplemented and extended by the possibility of
using the selecting potentialities of appropriately designed
equipment to conduct searches directed to those combinations
of concepts that are not explicitly set up in one of the arrays
of index entries and their subheadings. Achieving maximum
advantages from these capabilities of automatic equipment
requires (1) careful analysis both of previously recognized
information requirements and of possible unrealized applications of information and (2) interpretation of such analysis in
terms of procedures and systems, especially of carefully
formulated indexing policies for making use of well defined
headings, subheadings and related coding methods. The possibilities of applying appropriately designed automatic equipment
transcend the scope of alphabetical indexing and require a
more fundamental consideration of the analysis and correlation
of recorded information.

CHAPTER V

CORRELATION OF METHODS AND SYSTEMS

Attention has been directed to certain basic principles in
Chapter II and III and to various cost factors in Chapter IV,
not to attempt to prove that some one method or system is
"the" solution to the problem of selecting and correlating
recorded information. The diversity of information requirements, the variations in the parameters that characterize
recorded knowledge and the differences in circumstances
encountered in practical situations make it unthinkable that
any one system can hope to provide optimum benefits at all
times. In fact, the attempt to apply some one procedure or
method, without regard to variations in information requirements, the nature of the information involved and the practical
circumstances, is certain to lead to situations at least as
inefficient and grotesque as attempting to achieve all forms
of transportation with amphibious trucks. The decision as to
which methods or systems shall be used to meet practical
requirements have been rendered more difficult by the introduction of new capabilities and potentialities as the result of
the development of specially designed automatic equipment for
searching, storing, and correlating recorded information. If,
however, success crowns our efforts to apply such equipment
in an efficient fashion, the reward will be a very important
improvement--technical break-through--in our ability to
search, to select, to correlate and to utilize recorded information.

Before using our mathematical model to present a correlating review of various methods and procedures, it should
be emphasized that this model has been set up so as to permit
us to center our attention on various operations that can be
formulated as well-defined routines. Such operations constitute those activities that can be performed advantageously by
various clerical routines or automatic devices. Hence it is
necessary that we give careful attention to such operations

when considering how best to apply the various systems or
devices. It must not be forgotten, however, that providing
efficient means for accomplishing routine operations may
prove ineffective in dealing with recorded information unless
we are successful in coping with problems in the realm of
definition of terminology and the analysis of relationships
between terms both in a lexicographical sense (definition of
terms) and in a syntactical sense (relationships set up between
terms when recording and correlating observations and events).

Our mathematical model (Chapter II) has enabled us to
investigate certain consequences that arise in situations in
which we must deal with a large number of objects whose
characteristics enable them to be distinguished (by differences
in characteristics) and also to be grouped together (on the
basis of characteristics common to a plurality of objects). The
model led us to the conclusion that, with increase in the number of categories of characteristics, the number of ways in
which they may be combined becomes larger very rapidly.
Each combination of characteristics defines a class of objects.

In the general case there are no a priori reasons for
assuming that any one combination of characteristics--that
is to say, any one group of objects in our model--would be
more useful or important than another. Thus, in our model
system we have a situation in which we have imposed no re-
strictions of a priori importance of usefulness on any particular combination of characteristics. In discussing our model,
we also pointed out that special names could be assigned to
groups of objects each of which possesses some set of characteristics. If some one name applies to a broader range of
objects than another, then the first name may be said to be
more generic than the second. If the classes of objects designated by two names both embrace one or more of the same
objects, then the names are increasingly synonymous in character as the fraction of common objects increases. In other
words, we may define synonymity between two terms by the
degree to which two classes both include the same objects.

Naming objects and classifying them were thus shown to
have much in common. There is also much in common between (1) the definition of a class and (2) the formulation of
a concept and the corresponding definition of a word or term.

Although these conclusions were illustrated by analysis of our mathematical model based on the logical product type of relationship between characteristics, it was pointed out that logical sum and logical difference may also be involved in establishing combinations of basic characteristics when defining either classes of objects or corresponding terminology.

These observations and conclusions have been summarized so as to facilitate correlative review of various methods and procedures that have been applied or developed for identifying documents of pertinent interest to a given problem or situation. All these methods operate by taking cognizance of the characteristics of the documents during a preparatory analytical phase, recording the results of such analysis in various forms and then, during the searching-utilization phase, employing the results of the preparatory analysis to select--or to aid in the selection of--those documents of pertinent interest to a given problem or situation.

The various documentation methods thus have the common purpose of directing attention to a class of documents, namely those of pertinent interest to a given problem or situation. To achieve this purpose, they make use of the characteristics of the subject contents of documents. The devices and procedures used by the various documentation methods are sufficiently different that the methods vary considerably in capabilities and limitations. They also differ widely in cost of operation and in ability to meet various kinds of information requirements. These latter differences are, obviously, of great practical importance.

A. Classification

(1) Compartmentalized Classification

As already noted, the purpose of various documentation methods is to direct attention to a class of documents of pertinent interest to a given problem or situation. One approach to serving this purpose is to conduct the preparatory analytical processing of the documents in such a way that they are arranged in fixed groups. This general method may be referred to as compartmentalized classification. Its limitations arise, first of all, from the fact that even a rather small number of characteristics, as exemplified by our mathematical model,

may generate, by combination, an enormously large number
of possible groupings. Practical considerations permit only
a small fraction of the totality of possible groupings to be
physically established as fixed groups. This statement remains true, as a little reflection makes apparent, even when
it becomes practical, with various types of equipment, to
establish, say, 10 to 100 times as many groupings as was
previously feasible. With this approach it is necessary, for
practical reasons during the preliminary processing phase,
to make a choice among the totality of possible groupings.

This necessity of making a narrowly limited choice among
the large totality of possible groupings means, in practical
terms, that future use of the subject contents of documents
must be accurately forecast. More specifically, if this
approach is to function efficiently and satisfactorily, it must
be possible to express future information requirements as a
limited set of combinations of the characteristics of the document subject contents. Here two different kinds of difficulties
may be encountered. In the first place, the diverse character
of future information requirements may prevent them from
being brought into correspondence with a limited set of combinations of characteristics. In other words, future information requirements may correspond to a very large number of
different combinations of characteristics. A Procrustean bed
situation may thus arise and make this approach ineffective
and inadvisable. In the second place, it is often difficult to
forecast information requirements accurately and thus to be
able to meet the requirement that a narrow selection be made
among the enormously large number of possible combinations
of characteristics.

In practical situations, certain circumstances may be
favorable to compartmentalized classification. Certain combinations of characteristics such as function, form, dimen-
sions, material of construction, may be so obviously important that establishing useful groupings may be relatively simple.
Thus, for example, a housewife may encounter little difficulty
in establishing a classification of kitchen utensils and tableware. Such favorable circumstances may prevail when large
number of objects are involved, as in classifying nuts, bolts
and similar mechanical parts. Even in more complex situa-

tions, subdivisions into general categories may be effective
in establishing groupings whose specificity may not be sufficient to direct attention to items of pertinent interest but
whose utility achieves importance in avoiding the necessity
of dealing in a detailed fashion with most of the groupings.

In those instances in which it is possible to predict information requirements in terms of a limited number of combinations of characteristics, compartmentalized classification
offers the advantage of a relatively simple method. Simple
devices, e. g., a set of pigeonholes, may be used to establish
such a classification. However, other considerations, e. g.,
storage costs, may lead to the application of more elaborate
equipment

(2) Universal Decimal Classification

The limitations of compartmentalized classification, as
outlined above, have been recognized for many years. It was
observed that it was particularly difficult to establish a compartmentalized classification so that each of a large collection
of documents would be assigned to a single compartment or
(to say the same thing in other words) so that some one preestablished set of combinations of characteristics would correspond to the various combinations of characteristics of the
subject contents of the various documents. Instead of a single
set of combinations of characteristics--as would correspond
to one of the possible classification systems of our mathematical model of chapter II--a number of different combinations
of characteristics, would be set up, as might be exemplified
by logical product combinations, e. g., "Roman numeral VI,
letter D", or "sphere, gold, 4 inch diameter". These combinations not only constitute classificatory subdivisions in
their own right but, by the use of a plurality of such combinations, the subject contents of documents can be designated in
a more flexible fashion than with the pigeon-hole type of
classification that assigns each document to some one compartment. The above illustrated type of combinations of
characteristics provides the basis for the Universal Decimal
Classification whose name is derived from the use of decimal
numbers to designate various combinations of characteristics.
Thus, in selecting documents, all those bearing a certain number or a certain combination of numbers may be selected. A

wide variety of simple or complex devices may be used to accomplish routine operations involved in performing such selections.

Systems, such as the Universal Decimal Classification, can be made to function in a considerably more flexible fashion than fixed compartment systems previously discussed. It may, however, not be immediately obvious that such systems as the Universal Decimal Classification are subject to severe limitations in their ability to select on the basis of characteristic combinations that have not been established previously. Thus, if the logical product combinations "Roman numeral IV, letter D" and "sphere, gold, 4 inch diameter" have been established, a selection of those items that are characterized by both combinations will obviously include only a fraction of those items that are characterized by the combination "gold, letter D". Such a selection would require that all items corresponding to this combination be brought together, including, for example, gold cubes, pyramids and other shapes. In the Universal Decimal Classification the preestablished combinations of characteristics are based, however, on their hierarchial subordination with the result that any one characteristics, e.g., "letter D" may be scattered among a large number of the subordinate combinations and thus the characteristic in question may be available with difficulty, if at all in a practical sense, for the generation of new combinations of characteristics, as required to meet unforeseen information requirements.

Stated in general terms, this approach is severely limited in its flexibility and effectiveness by the fact that it is based on a hierarchial subordination of different sets of categories one to another. Only those characteristics in categories that are at the top of the hierarchial combination can be used directly as a basis for effecting selection of documents to meet information requirements. The lower in the hierarchy a given category of characteristics is placed, the larger the number of subdivisions in which it appears, the more effort is required to use the category of characteristics in question for effecting the selection of pertinent documents. This practical limitation on the effectiveness of such a system becomes more severe, as is evident from our mathematical model, when the

number of categories of characteristics is larger and the range
of information requirements is more diverse.

However, in operating such a system, the above mentioned limitations may not be immediately apparent when the
number of documents embraced is relatively small. During
the earlier stages of practical operation, the system brings
to the user's attention relatively small numbers of documents
and little time is lost in reviewing the irrelevant. With larger
and larger numbers of documents, the situation deteriorates
steadily as the limitations on the flexibility and selective
power of such a system prevent it from making use of the
full range of combinations of characteristics in effecting selection. The result is that, for many information requirements, the user is flooded with large volumes of irrelevant
material. This type of frustration can lead the users to
restrict their inquiries to those kinds of information requirements that can be serviced by the system. Thus, in effect,
such a system can impose a certain pattern of utilization of
information on the user. He may, in effect, be very subtly
sabotaged in his use of an information file without even being
consciously aware of the fact.

It is also interesting to note that, in this type of system
as exemplified by the Universal Decimal Classification, the
characteristics used early in the history of the system to
generate classificatory combinations are, as a rule, generic
in character. As the limitations in flexibility, as outlined
above, begin to generate user frustrations, the latter often
lead to use of more specific terminology in an attempt to compensate for inability to provide selectivity by searching on the
basis of individual classification numbers or combinations of
such numbers. Such use of more specific terminology leads
to more and more highly ramified sets of subdivisions, sub-
subdivisions, etc. without overcoming the basic difficulty of
the system, namely, the arbitrary nature of the subordination
of one category of characteristics to others in such a way as
to cause the subordinate characteristics to be difficult to use
or even completely ineffective in forming combinations of
characteristics that correspond to search requirements. These
trends may be observed by studying the history of the evolution of the Universal Decimal Classification system and, more

especially, case histories of its application under varying
circumstances.

B.   Characterizing Systems

Up to this point, our review of systems on the basis of
our mathematical model has been concerned with systems in
which preestablished combinations of characteristics, mostly
generic in nature, have been used either to group documents
physically or to designate the nature and scope of their subject
contents. As we have seen, these methods are subject to
severe limitations whose origin may be traced (1) to the enor-
mous number of combinations that may be generated from a
modest number of characteristics and (2) to inability to predict
which combinations of characteristics will correspond to future
information requirements. The methods to be considered in
the remainder of this section make use of characteristics--
particularly those of more generic nature--in a much different
fashion.

(1) Alphabetized Indexing

A very common embodiment of this method type is alphabetized indexing. Considered from a general point of view,
this system provides an array of symbols, which, as a rule,
denote characteristics of a more specific (i. e., less generic)
nature. An appropriate rule (or rules) provides for the ordering of the symbols in such a way as to facilitate the location of
any one symbol in the array.

From the point of view of our mathematical model, an
alphabetized index consists of a series of words or terms, each
of which may be regarded as a derived characteristic which is
almost always of a low degree of generic character and which
may be regarded as derived from other more generic or basic
characteristics. In a certain sense, therefore, each heading
in a subject index corresponds to a classification subdivision,
whose low degree of generic character means that it will embrace a relatively small fraction of the total range of objects
within the system. In our mathematical model system any one
of an enormously large number of derived characteristics
could be generated from our set of basic characteristics. The
derived characteristics which constitute the building blocks of
alphabetized indexes may be regarded as selected from a very

large potential set of possible derived characteristics. Such
selection has been accomplished in part as the result of the
generation of language during the course of centuries and in
part as the result of the formulation of scientific and technical
concepts as a result of scientific research, industrial development and related activities. Thus, the derived characteristics
used in constructing subject indexes reflect the structure of
conceptualization both of everyday language and also of the
more specialized terminology of various areas of specialization. The building blocks of subject indexes are, as a consequence, usually based directly on those concepts in terms of
which the user of the index conducts his thinking. This general
rule does not mean that non-experts will be able to use such
specialized indexes as the molecular formula index of Chemical Abstracts.   To the chemist, however, this index is quite
readily understandable and, in this sense at least, in harmony
with his thought processes.

The limitations of alphabetized indexes and similar arrays
become important and also more apparent as the scope of an
information requirement become broader. With more generic
information requirements, the number of index entries that
have to be consulted increases, with a corresponding rise in
searching costs (see chapter IV). For locating individual
facts, e. g., in ascertaining a telephone number, an alphabetized index, as exemplified by the telephone directory, often
provides a large measure of advantage over other methods or
procedures for supplying information.

(2) Independently Recorded Characteristics

The above outlined limitations of conventional classification and of alphabetized indexes not only have impelled the
development of more flexible methods of search and correlating but have also provided guidance in conducting this development. It was widely recognized* a number of years ago, that
versatile information systems may be based on the principle
of independently recording various characteristics of the subject matter of documents and then directing selecting operations to combinations of characteristics or, much less

---

* See, for example, Perry, J. W. "Information Analysis for
  Machine Searching", American Documentation, 1, 133-9 (1950)

commonly, to various individual characteristics.

A rather wide variety of systems have been worked out on the basis of the above stated principles*. These systems have the following general operations in common:

(1) Analysis of the subject contents of graphic records in terms of characteristics. (Different systems vary markedly with respect to the range of characteristics that are employed, as discussed in more detail subsequently.)

(2) Recording the result of such analysis in some appropriate form. (The mode of recording of characteristics is at least strongly influenced by the devices or means employed to effect selection, as noted under 4 below.)

(3) Analysis of an information requirement in terms of its characteristics. (Such analysis is a necessary and obvious preliminary to accomplishing the next step.)

(4) Selection of items of pertinent interest by matching the characteristics of the graphic records with the characteristics of the information requirement. (This selecting operation may be formulated as a more or less complex sequence of logically defined operations. A wide variety of devices, equipment and procedures have been developed and applied successfully to accomplishing this selection operation. For example, the selecting operation may be accomplished as a clerical routine based on matching of numbers. More commonly, however, the selecting operation is accomplished by various devices such as hand-sorted punched cards, IBM machines or specially designed searching and selecting equipment.)

(a) Hand-sorted Punched Cards

It is perhaps obvious from this summary that policy as to the selection and definition of the characteristics on which

* See, especially, Hyslop, Marjorie R., "Inventory of Methods and Devices for Analysis, Storage and Retrieval of Information", Chapter VI in "Documentation in Action" edited by Jesse H. Shera, Allen Kent and J. W. Perry, Reinhold Publishing Corp., New York, 1956.

analysis is to be based may vary widely. It may be decided,
for example, to base the analysis of subject matter on a re-
stricted list of carefully defined, rather generic characteristics. This approach offers certain advantages particularly
when dealing with a narrow range of subject matter and with
relatively small files, e.g., ten thousand items or less. A
small number of characteristics, e.g., 100-500, may be
recorded independently, as required to designate important
aspects of subject matter, on hand-sorted punched cards.
These cards may then be subjected to sorting and selecting
operations directed to such combinations of characteristics as
may correspond to information requirements. Experience has
shown that manually manipulated punched cards have two prin-
cipal limitations that tend to restrict their usefulness to small
files. First, manual sorting becomes more time consuming
and tedious as the file becomes larger. Second, the number
of characteristics that may be recorded by punching any one
card is limited and, as a consequence, the selectivity is also
limited. Many ingenious methods have been worked out for
exploiting the capabilities of marginally punched cards, but
none of these methods can be said to surmount both of these
limitations.

(b) Aspect Cards

With hand-sorted punched cards, all of the characteristics
used to designate the subject contents of a single document are
recorded on a single card. Searching operations may then be
directed to any one of these characteristics or to any combination of the latter that may be appropriate to a given information
requirement. The basic principle of "one card, one document"
may be, in effect, reversed so that a different card is assigned
to each characteristic. The various documents to which a
given characteristic pertains are then registered on the characteristic card, e.g., by punching certain positions or by writing numbers on the card. A search to a combination of characteristics is then performed by comparing the punching or the
written entries on the cards for the characteristics that make
up the combination. Searches directed to combinations of the
logical product type are easily and quickly performed but
searches based on combinations involving logical sums and
differences, if at all complex, may become tedious or difficult.

Furthermore, this approach encounters difficulties and practical limitations in registering relationships between generic and specific concepts and this tends to lead to difficulties in making simultaneous use of specific and generic characteristics for analysis of subject contents. Furthermore, this approach does not permit syntactical relationships (for example a substance to its properties, or a process to accompanying conditions) to be registered conveniently for use in conducting searching and selecting operations. These limitations become more apparent as the number of documents embraced by such a system becomes very large. One of the advantages of the system--the possibility of providing a separate card for each characteristic--has presented, to some persons using this approach, an irresistible temptation to use words as found in documents as the characteristics to be registered. It is, of course, possible to operate in this fashion, as a separate card (or similar recording unit) can be set up for each word. On the other hand, disregard of synonyms, near-synonyms and differences in degree of generic character among different terms must inevitably reduce the reliability of selection and correlation that can be accomplished.

(c) Machine Manipulation of Characteristics

Enough has been said, perhaps, to make the point that selection of a given device, machine or set of equipment will strongly influence the extent to which various characteristics may be used to effect searching, selecting, and correlating operations. This is perhaps most obvious for hand-sorted punched cards, but the same statement is true of punched cards manipulated by automatic accounting equipment and also of large scale computers such as Univac or the IBM 700 series. The design of automatic accounting equipment is such that detection of a characteristic during searching operations requires that it be recorded by punching in a predetermined position on the cards. This restriction imposes such severe limitations on the ability to record characteristics, that accounting type equipment has proved useful mainly in narrowly defined fields, such as infrared spectroscopic data or patents on additives to petroleum products. With Univac and similar computers, their design is such that programming selecting operations is rendered time-consuming and

difficult*. Furthermore, the accomplishment of the complex
routines that are made necessary by virtue of the equipment's
design results in slowing the effective operating speeds to a
surprising degree. The difficulty in this connection, it should
be emphasized, is not the nature of selection operations, which
are inherently simple in nature. Rather, the difficulty is in
the design of presently available commercial computers. By
proper design of the electrical circuits, high-speed searching
equipment can be constructed for a fraction of the cost of a
Univac or an IBM 700 series computer and the programming
can be reduced to wiring a plugboard--an operation that can be
accomplished, on the average, in ten minutes to an hour depending on the complexity of the search to be performed.

This brief discussion of equipment has been presented to
make the point that the selection (and also the design) of equipment must be based on such engineering considerations as
purposes and requirements as well as machine capabilities and
costs. The situation might be summarized by stating that a
given device, machine or set of equipment provides certain
capabilities and these must be aligned with purposes and requirements in order to provide an optimum margin of benefits
over costs.

In this connection, it is also important to emphasize that
the capabilities provided by a given device, machine or set of
equipment require, for effective functioning, that information
be analyzed as to its characteristics. For situations in which
a maximum of discriminating and correlating power is advantageous, the cost of conducting detailed analysis may be held
to a low point by applying the methods of encoded abstracts.
This method has been worked out so as to achieve the maximum
degree of consistency in the analysis of complex subject

---

* For detailed analysis of this point, see Bagley, P. R.,
"Electronic Digital Machines for High-Speed Information
Searching", Master's theses, MIT, August, 1951, also Report
R-200, Digital Computer Laboratory, MIT, November, 1951.
Recent discussions with IBM and Sperry-Rand personnel
indicate that the conclusions of the Bagley thesis apply to
commercially available computers developed during the past
five years.

matter*. To conduct searching and correlating operations based on encoded abstracts, the selecting capabilities described recently in <u>Applied Mechanics Reviews</u> would be appropriate. **

It should be noted that the encoded abstract method of analyzing the subject matter of documents permits selection to be based, not only on substantive aspects, such as the designation of objects, persons, locations, attributes, processes and conditions but also on relationships of a syntactical nature, as exemplified by the relationship of a substance to its properties or of a process to attendant conditions. In this way, the encoded abstract method provides the highest degree of discriminating and correlating power developed to the present time. As discussed in the next section, the encoding of abstracts may be coordinated with the preparation of abstract bulletins or similar digests. Thus, analysis of information for searching, selecting and retrieval may be coordinated with processing to serve other purposes, especially current awareness.

It is not intended to suggest that the encoded abstract procedure will always provide optimum advantages under all circumstances. As already noted, hand-sorted punched cards and equipment designed for accounting have been applied to advantage in narrow fields of specialization.

In concluding this section, it should be noted that consistency in the characterization of subject matter is essential to attaining reliable results regardless of the method, system or device that may be used. For example, when using compartmentalized classification it is highly important that the scope of each class and subclass be defined with precision. Meeting this requirement to ensure reliable results leads to the necessity of careful definition of terminology, as is attested, for

---

* A. Kent, R. E. Booth, and J. W. Perry, "Machine Searching of Metallurgical Literature, <u>Metal Progress</u>, February 1957. See also J. W. Perry, A. Kent, and M. M. Berry, "Machine Literature Searching", Interscience Publishers, New York, 1956.

**J. W. Perry and A. Kent, "The New Look in Library Science", <u>Applied Mechanics Reviews</u>, 9, No. 11, 457-60 (Nov. 1956).

example, by the classification bulletins of the U. S. Patent Office. In alphabetized indexing, the control of terminology in general and possibilities of confusion from synonyms and near-synonyms require special care and attention. A carelessly constructed index can be a trap for the unwary or a source of exasperation and frustration for the discriminating user. Similarly, when using less orthodox or more complex devices, consistency in the analysis of information, especially careful attention to the use of synonyms and generic terminology, is the key to achieving reliability in searching, selecting and correlating. In exceptional circumstances, when reliability of performance is of minor importance, it may be permissible to relax the rule of care in use of terminology and base the analysis of information on the indiscriminate use of the words encountered in documents. The degree of confusion thereby engendered is sometimes underestimated, with inevitable resultant difficulties in making efficient use of recorded information.

CHAPTER VI

RESUME OF SYSTEMS DESIGN

Attention so far has been devoted to methods and procedures for identifying documents containing information of pertinent interest to a given problem or situation. Such emphasis
on identification and related searching operations appeared
advisable for two reasons: (1) Limitations in the ability to
identify pertinent documents in large files often imposes a
ceiling on the usefulness of the information that they contain.
(2) A very large improvement in our ability to search and to
identify appears attainable by application of various types of
newly developed equipment. At the same time, specialized
equipment which greatly compresses the storage size of documents can make a contribution of great practical importance
in eliminating or at least greatly reducing storage problems
encountered with large files. Not only can storage costs be
reduced, but accessibility to large files can be improved.

In planning and establishing systems for applying various
types of equipment, it should not be assumed that a selection
is to be made once and for all of some one "best" indexing,
classifying or coding method. Such an approach would, in
effect, overlook the capabilities of various systems and automatic equipment. Rather it must be realized that capabilities
and potentialities of various systems are such that a wide
variety of indexing, classifying and coding procedures can be
accomplished by applying them. Which procedure--or combination of procedures--will be most advantageous will depend
on various factors of which the more important are the purposes to be served, the nature of the information, including
the format of the graphic records, the number of the latter,
desired reliability of retrieval, and urgency requirements.

An additional aspect of general information requirements
is the provision of current awareness of newly acquired
material. This requirement is sometimes referred to as the
"newspaper function", in order to emphasize its distinctly

different character from the filing, storage and use of large numbers of documents, sometimes termed the "archive function". To serve the newspaper function, the preparation and distribution of multiple copies of numerous reports is often necessary.

In a similar way, a central file may serve as a general pool of information from which, by selection procedures, subsidiary files may be derived to meet interim situations or to serve specialized requirements on a continuing basis.

Consideration of capabilities of various systems and equipment does not suffice, of course, to work out a system of methods and procedures to meet a given set of circumstances. In working out a large-scale system, organizational considerations would require attention, as well as the more technical questions of appropriate indexing, coding, searching and correlating procedures. Organizational considerations might result, for example, in establishing a centralized information operation with responsibilities to collect, and to process various documents in order to provide various services. Such services might include, (1) prompt distribution of copies of documents relating to certain subjects to various specialists or specialized organizations, (2) selecting from accumulated files documents of pertinent interest to specific information requirements, (3) preparing summary reports on situations or problems that require attention, (4) establishing subsidiary files. This list of services is intended to be illustrative and suggestive rather than definitive or exhaustive.

Provision of information services on a centralized basis makes necessary decisions as to·the extent of centralization and, in particular, which operations are to be centralized and which are not. Here again, a specific set of procedures cannot be established on the basis of the capabilities of available equipment. Rather, a careful study of requirements and circumstances is necessary before a set of operating procedures can be specified.

In this connection it may be helpful, perhaps, to point out some of the possibilities for achieving efficiency and economy. To this end the following outline is included in this chapter.

To facilitate our presentation, the processing of informa-

tion preparatory to distribution, storage and subsequent
retrieval will be considered to occur in two main steps:
- (a) analysis of the recorded information;
- (b) recording the results of this analysis in a form
  which will suit the particular searching and
  retrieval equipment available.

The first step (analysis) almost always requires perusal
and understanding of records and consequently this step is a
costly one. Fortunately this step can be conducted in such a
way that an economical majority of the requirements of potential users are taken into account by the generation of a single,
highly stylized abstract. *

The results of the single analysis may then be utilized in
a number of ways, as shown in Figure 40.

It is seen from this figure that a thorough, stylized abstract contains sufficient information to permit communication
to the reader when published either in conventional form (I) or
in telegraphic form (II). Similarly, the stylized abstract
facilitates the selection of index entries, aspects, subject
headings, and codes for one or more of the various types of
information retrieval systems (III). For searching operations
having high discriminating and correlating capabilities, the
entire stylized abstract may be translated into code form either
by clerical routines or by automatic procedures.

The stylized abstract may be recorded in legible form, to
provide two basic services: Namely, current awareness, or,
the "newspaper" function (V), and retrospective searching, or
the "archive function", (VII). For the former purpose, copies
of abstracts may be distributed at frequent intervals, e.g.,
weekly, and, for the latter purpose, selected abstracts, recorded on unit records, may be provided. In meeting both

---

* S. N. Alexander, National Bureau of Standards: talk pre-
sented at Officers' Club, Bolling Field, Washington, D. C.,
February 12, 1957. Cf. A. Kent and J. W. Perry, "New
Indexing-Abstracting System for Formal Reports, Develop-
ment and Proof Services, Aberdeen Proving Ground",
American Documentation, 8, No. 1, 34-46 (1957).

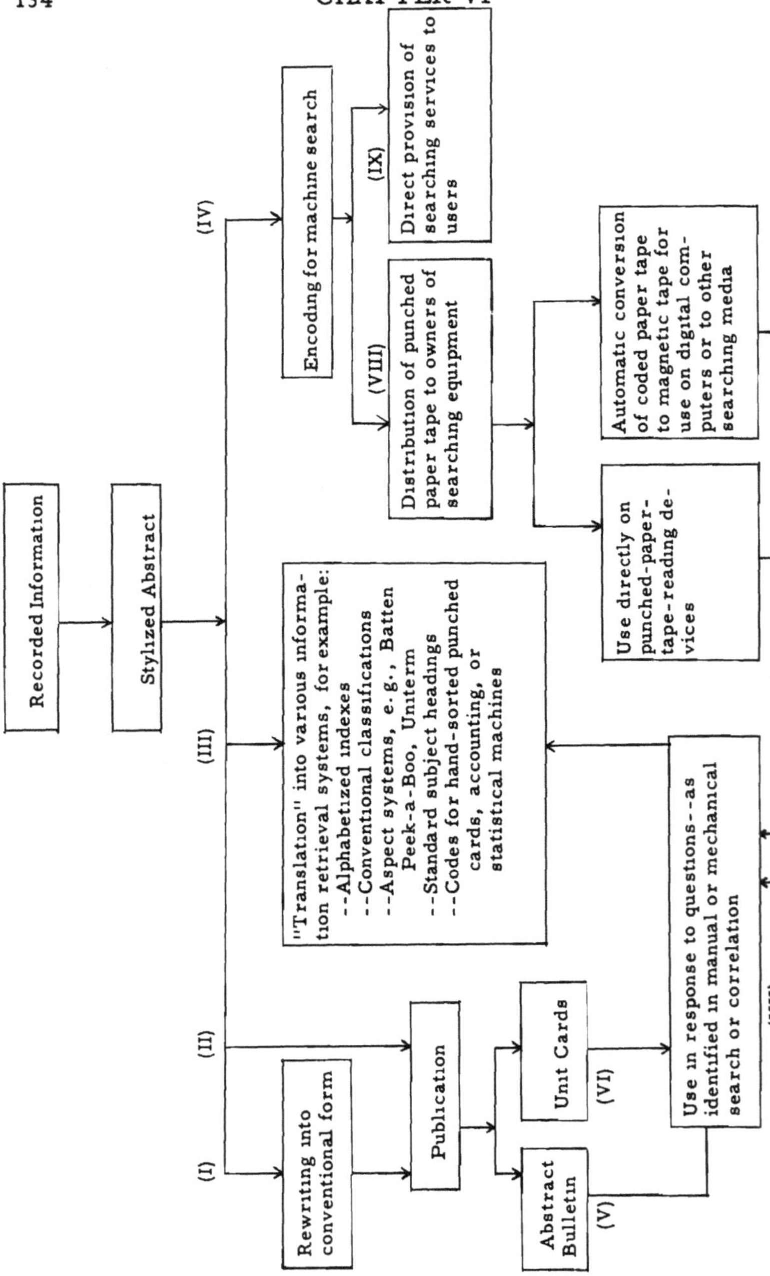

Figure 40. Multiple Uses of Single Analysis of Recorded Information

purposes, it may prove advantageous to provide copies of the original documents with the abstracts.

When the abstract has been encoded it becomes effective in two services related to the archive function, namely: providing a searching service in response to specific demand (IX); and providing all or selected portions of the total file to offices or organizations equipped with searching equipment (VIII) in order that they may be able to conduct their own searches, perhaps coordinated with internal, confidential organizational reports which have been encoded in a similar manner.

GLOSSARY

This glossary consists mainly of terms defined in a paper, on "The Jargon of Machine Literature Searching" by T. H. Rees, Jr., and Allen Kent. This paper was presented before the 131st meeting of the American Chemical Society, Miami, Florida, April 11, 1957. Terms preceded by an asterisk (*) are taken from J. Mack, and R. S. Taylor, Chapter I in "Documentation in Action," edited by J. H. Shera, Allen Kent, and J. W. Perry, Reinhold, New York, 1956.

*Alphabetic Coding. A system of abbreviations used in preparing information for input into a machine, such that information may be reported not only in numbers but also in letters and words. For example, Boston, New York, Philadelphia, Washington, may in alphabetical coding be reported as BS, NY, PH, WA.

*Analytico-Synthetic Classification. A classification which represents a subject by analyzing it into its fundamental constituent elements, and synthesizing a class symbol for the subject out of these elements linked by appropriate connecting symbols.

Analytic Relationship. The relationship which exists between concepts (and corresponding terms) by virtue of their definition and inherent scope of meaning.

Array. A set of symbols or documents arranged in order by some rule, for example, symbols representing the set of mutually exclusive coordinate subclasses totally exhaustive of a class.

Aspect cards. Cards on which are entered the accession

numbers of documents in an information retrieval system
which are judged to be related in an important fashion to
the concept for which the card is established. See also
Peek-a-boo Cards, Uniterm Cards, Index Entry,
Uniterm system, Docuterm, Descriptor.

Association Trails. Linkages between two or more documents
or items of information, based on the results of their examination and recorded for personal or automatic detection.

Automatic Coding.   Any technique in which a mechanical or
electrical device (or devices) is used to help bridge the
gap between some "easiest" form, intellectually and
manually, of describing the steps to be followed in solving
a given problem and some "most efficient" final coding of
the same problem for a given computer. Two basic operations often involved are dictionary look-up and symbol
encoding. See also Automatic Dictionary.

Automatic Dictionary.   (1) The fundamental component of a
translating machine which will provide a   routine, unse-
lected word for word substitution from one language to
another.   (2) In automatic searching systems, the automatic dictionary is the component which substitutes codes
for words or phrases during the encoding operation. See
also Automatic coding.

*Automatic Programming (Computers). Any technique whereby
the computer itself is used to transform programming
from a form that results from human problem analysis into
a form that is efficient for the computer to carry out.
Examples of automatic programming are compiling routines, interpretive routines, etc.

Barriers.   Symbols used to separate the various syntactical
levels (e. g., "words", "phrases", "sentences") of a
telegraphic abstract.

Batten system.   See Peek-a-boo system.

*Binary Digit.   A digit in the binary scale of notation. This
digit may be only 0 (zero) or 1 (one). It is equivalent to
an "on condition" or an "off condition", a "yes" or a "no",
etc.

*Binary Notation. The writing of numbers in the scale of two.
The first dozen numbers zero to eleven are written 0, 1,
10, 11, 100, 101, 110, 111, 1000, 1001, 1010, 1011. The
positions of the digits designate powers of two; thus 1010
means 1 times two cubed or eight, 0 times two squared
or four, 1 times two to the first power or two, and 0
times two to the zero power or one; this is equal to one
eight plus no four's plus one two plus no ones, which is
ten.

*Bit. (from Binary digit). A unit of measure of information
consisting of the amount transmitted or stored by the
choice of one out of a possible two signals.

Boolean Algebra. The science of symbols denoting logical
propositions and their combination according to certain
rules which correspond to the laws of logic.

Brussels Classification. See Universal Decimal Classification.

*Character. (1) One of a set of elementary symbols such as
those corresponding to the keys on a typewriter. The
symbols may include the decimal digits 0 through 9, the
letters A through Z, punctuation marks, operation symbols, any any other single symbols which a computer may
read, store, or write. (2) A pulse-code representation
of such a symbol.

Characteristic. An aspect, subject, idea, concept or
element of description which is applicable to the content
of a graphic record and which may be useful for future
identification of the record.

Classification. An orderly arrangement of terms developed
by division of a subject by means of a train of characteristics. Extended to mean any form of systematically
arranged subject matter. Further extended to mean an
artificial language of ordinal numbers designed to mechan-
ize this arrangement.

*Code. Any system of symbols in the communication process.
Particularly a system which achieves abbreviation or
some other desirable advantage over common language
or numerical expression.

Code Dictionary. An alphabetical arrangement of English words and terms, associated with their code representations. See also Reverse Code Dictionary.

Coding. Any system of symbols in the communication process, particularly a system which achieves abbreviation, consistency of expression, ease of representation, or some other desirable advantages over common language or numerical expression.

Colon Classification. A system developed by S. R. Ranganathan, in which documents are analyzed by such generic concepts (facets) as "method", "problem", "variable", and "space". A special notation has been developed for this system.

Concept Coordination. A term used to describe the basic principles of various punched card, aspect, and mechanized information retrieval systems which involve the multidimensional analysis of information and coordinate retrieval. In concept coordination, independently assigned concepts are used to characterize the subject contents of documents and the latter are identified during searching by means of either such assigned concepts or combination of the same.

Coordinate Indexing. (This term sometimes used synomously with "Uniterm System", which see). A method for independently designating the characteristics of graphic records so that they may be identified and selected by designating combinations of characteristics.

Cordonnier system. See Peek-a-boo system.

Correlation. The process of relating one set of measurements to another or of drawing together various facts, particularly for the purpose of attaining insight into otherwise obscure situations.

Cross-reference. A notation which makes explicit a relationship between two or more graphic records, or between two or more portions of an information retrieval system.

*Cybernetics. Comparative study of the control system formed by the nervous system and the brain and mechanoelectrical communication systems, such as computing machines.

*Data Processor. A machine for handling information in a sequence of logically defined operations.

Derived Characteristic. A characteristic (which see) which consists of a combination of two or more, more basic characteristics (logical product); one or more of several more basic characteristics (logical sum); or one or more of several more basic characteristics in which the absence of one or more, more basic characteristics is specified (logical difference).

Descriptor. An index entry used to characterize a document. See also Index Entry, Uniterm Cards, Aspect Cards.

*Digital Computer. A computer which calculates using numbers expressed in digits and yeses and noes expressed usually in 1's and 0's, to represent all the variables that occur in a problem.

*Direct Code. In punched cards, a direct code uses a single hole to represent a single idea.

Disjunctive Search. A search defined in terms of a logical sum (which see).

Document. An arbitrary unit of recorded knowledge which furnishes information upon a subject. A graphic record (which see) or group of such records which are physically bound together or otherwise contained or attached so that it may be recognized as a single object. Examples of documents are books, reports, letters, films, photographs, and tape recordings.

*Documentation. The group of techniques necessary for the orderly presentation, organization and communication of recorded specialized knowledge, in order to give maximum accessibility and utility to the information contained.

Docuterm. The combination of (a) a word or phrase considered to be important for later retrieval of information and (b) a Role Indicator (which see).

Encoded Question. A question set up and encoded in a form

appropriate for operating, programming or conditioning a searching device.

External Memory (Computers). Materials separate from the computer itself but holding information stored in language acceptable to the machine, as for example, recorded magnetic or punched paper tape in a closet, photographic film on reels, or punch cards in filing cabinets.

E-Z Sort Card. A marginal punched-card manufactured by E-Z Sort, Ltd., of San Francisco, California.

False coordination. See False Drops and Noise.

False Drops. Documents spuriously identified as pertinent by an information retrieval system, but which do not satisfy the search requirements, due to improper coding, or to spurious combinations of holes punched using random, superimposed coding, or improper use of terminology. See also Noise.

*Feedback. The partial reversion of the effects of a given process to its source or to a preceding stage so as to reinforce or modify it.

Field. (1) Punched-card Machines. A set of one or more columns in each of a number of punched cards which is regularly used to report a standard item of information. For example, if columns 16 and 19 are regularly used to report weekly rate of pay, then these columns would constitute a field. (2) Computers. A set of one or more characters (not necessarily all lying in the same word) which is treated as a whole; a unit of information.

File. A collection of documents or other graphic records containing information which is judged to be of possible future interest.

Filmorex. An information-retrieval machine invented by Dr. Jacques Samain which records on a single piece of photographic film both codes (indexing entries, classification numbers, etc.) as well as a microimage of a paper abstract, photograph, etc. Selection is effected by conditioning the machine in terms of one code per search. The pieces of film are scanned photoelectrically.

Fixed Fields. A field (which see) in computers, film selection devices, or punched cards or a given number of holes
along the edge of a marginal punched card, set aside, or
"fixed", for the recording of a given type of characteristic.

Free Fields. A property of information retrieval devices
which permits recording of information in the search
medium without regard to preassigned fixed fields (which
see). See also Random, superimposed coding.

Generic Characteristic. A characteristic (which see) which
applies to a greater number of graphic records or objects
than a specific characteristic.

Generic Coding. The encoding of terms in such a way that
more generic aspects of the terms are made explicit for
searching.

Graphic Record. A medium, such as paper, film, tape, etc.
which contains information of any kind which is either
temporarily or permanently recorded thereon.

Index Entry. A word or term, with or without a modifying or
limiting phrase, by which a document is characterized.
As usually arranged in an alphabetical array the word or
term is associated with the page or document number to
which the entry pertains. See, Aspect Cards, Descriptor,
Uniterm System, Docuterm, and others for definitions and
connotations that have much in common with "Index Entry".

Indexing. The process of selecting or formulating an index
entry. See also Uniterming, Word Indexing.

Information Requirements. Actual or anticipated questions
which may be posed to an information retrieval system
(which see).

Information Retrieval. The recovering of desired information
or data from a collection of documents or other graphic
records.

Information Retrieval System. A system for locating and
selecting, on demand, certain documents, or other
graphic records relevant to a given information requirement from a file of such material. Examples of informa-

tion retrieval systems are classification, indexing and
machine searching systems.

Information Theory.   The mathematical concept of the transmission of information developed by Shannon and Weaver.

Interfix.   An arbitrary symbol or serial number assigned to
two or more codes to indicate a relationship between the
codes.   See also Barriers and Role Indicators.

*Internal Memory (Computers).   The total memory or storage
which is accessible automatically to the computer without
human intervention.   This component is an integral physical part of the computer and is directly controlled by the
computer.

Keysort Cards.   A brand of marginal punched-cards made
by the Royal-McBee Company of Athens, Ohio.

Logical difference.   Given two classes a and b, the logical
difference a - b consists of all elements belonging to
class a but not to class b.

*Logical Product.   Given two classes a and b, the logical prod-
uct or intersect, ab, consists of those elements belonging
both to class a and to class b.

*Logical Sum.   Given two classes a and b, the union or logical
sum, a + b, consists of all elements belonging to either a
or b or both.

Luhn Scanner.   An experimental IBM machine, invented by
H. P. Luhn, which photoelectrically scanned punched
cards which were fed through the machine end-on. Appropriate wiring of the plugboard permitted searches based
on logical products, sums, and differences to be made.

Machine Language.   A system for interpreting and coding
information to make it amenable to machine processing.

Machine Translation.   The automatic interpretation of recorded information from one language to another.   See also
Automatic Dictionary.

*Machine Word (Computers).   A unit of information represented
by a number of characters, which a digital computer reg-

ularly handles in each transfer. For example, a machine may regularly handle numbers or instructions in units of 36 binary digits which constitute a machine word.

Mathematical Model. The general characterization of a process, object, or concept, in terms of mathematics, which enables the relatively simple manipulation of variables to be accomplished in order to determine how the process, object, or concept would behave in different situations.

McBee Card. See Keysort Card.

Memex. A hypothetical machine described by Vannevar Bush, which would store written records so that they would be available almost instantly by merely pushing one or more control buttons.

*Memory (Computers). The unit or units which store information in a form that may be scanned by machines to initiate or to control automatic operations. (2) Any device into which information can be introduced and then extracted at a later time.

Minicard. A machine developed by the Eastman Kodak Co. which stores coded information on small pieces of film, each of which contains codes for index entries, classification numbers etc., for the document, in the form of light and dark spots. Microimages of the document may also be recorded together with codes on the pieces of film.

Multiaspect. Said of searches or systems which permit more than one aspect (or facet) of information to be used in combination to effect identifying and selecting operations.

Multiaspect System. An information-retrieval system in which the characteristics of graphic records judged to be important for subsequent retrieval are recorded independently so as to permit more than one aspect of information to be used in combination to effect identifying or selecting operations. See also Characteristic.

Multiple Searches. Two or more searches performed simultaneously. See also Multiplexing.

Multiplexing.   Transmission of a number of different mes-
sages simultaneously over a single circuit. See also
Multiple Searches.

Mutually Exclusive Characteristics. A set of characteristics
(which see) in which the specification of a characteristic
from a given set to generate a combination of characteristics excludes the possibility of other characteristics
from the same set being specified with the combination
in question.

Noise.   In the Shannon-Weaver information theory, spurious ,
and extraneous signals, introduced randomly. See also
False Drops.

Noise Factor. The fraction of documents to which attention is
directed which are found, on inspection, to be not pertinent. $\frac{M-W}{M}$, where M = number of documents which use
of a given literature searching system indicates to be of
possible pertinent interest, and W = number of documents
found to be of actual pertinent interest, upon inspection of
the M documents. See also Pertinency Factor.

Numerical-Code. A coding system for punched cards whereby
aspects of information are assigned numbers, which are
punched into the card, using, for example, a 7-4-2-1 code.

*Operations Research.   (Operational Research) A systematic
method utilizing the analysis of statistics for studying and
improving the operations of men and machines.

*Output (Computers).   (1) Information transferred from the
internal storage of a computer to secondary or external
storage.   (2) Information transferred to any device exter-
ior to the computer.

*Parameter (Computers).   In a subroutine, a quantity which
may be given different values when the subroutine is used
in different parts of one main routine, but which usually
remains unchanged throughout any one such use. To use
a subroutine successfully in many different programs
requires that the subroutine be adaptable by changing its
parameters.

Peek-a-boo Cards. Cards into which holes are punched in

specific locations to represent accession numbers of
documents in an information retrieval system. Each
card corresponds to an aspect of information and the
punching indicates which documents are judged to pertain
to the aspect for which the card is established. Variations of this type of card are Batten and Cordonnier cards.
See also Aspect Cards.

Peek-a-boo System. An information retrieval system which
uses peek-a-boo cards (which see). Cards representing
the aspects of information of interest in a search are
superimposed. The holes which coincide (through which
light passes) serve to locate the numbers of documents
which relate to all the aspects of interest.

Pertinency Factor. The fraction of documents to which attention is directed which are found, upon inspection, to be
pertinent. $\frac{W}{M}$, where W and M are defined under the term
noise factor. See also Noise Factor, Recall Factor,
Resolution Factor.

Photoelectric Scanning. Scanning of punched cards by photoelectric means, as opposed to the electrical brushes or
"feelers," or mechanical plungers. See Luhn Scanner.

Pigeon-hole Classification. Grouping of similar documents
into classes, separated physically into compartments or
similarly isolated locations.

Plugboard. The control board of an automatic device which
is conditioned by appropriate wiring to control the various
machine functions.

Precoordination. In the Uniterm system, the combination of
individual words to form phrases. The phrases, analo-
gous to subject headings, are used to designate important
aspects of subject matter of documents. See also Uniterm system.

*Program (noun) (Computers). A plan for the solution of a
problem. A complete program includes plans for the
transcription of date, coding for the computer and plans
for the absorption of the results into the system. The
list of coded instructions is called a Routine (which see).

*Program (verb) (Computers).   To plan a computation or process from the read in of information to the delivery of the results, including the integration of the operation into an existing system.   Thus programming consists of planning and coding, including numerical analysis, systems analysis, specification of printing formats, and any functions necessary to the integration of a computer in a system.   See Code (noun).

*Punched Card.   (Also Punch Card) A data card with holes punched or notched in particular positions, each positioned hole having a particular assigned signification, for automatic sorting or computing with electrically operated tabulating or accounting equipment or with manually or mechanically manipulated devices.

Random, Superimposed Coding.   A system of coding in which a set of random numbers is assigned to each concept to be encoded.   With punched cards, each number corresponds to some one hole to be punched in a given Field (which see).   Several of the sets of random numbers may be recorded in the same field of a given card.   In order to prevent an unacceptably large number of False Drops (which see) during a search, the number of codes that may be recorded in a single field must be limited.   See also Direct Code, Numerical Code.

Rapid Selector. A device designed to scan codes recorded on microfilm.   Microimages of the documents associated with the codes may also be recorded on the film.

Recall Factor.   The fraction of pertinent documents to which the system directed attention. $\frac{W}{X}$, where W is defined under the term Noise Factor and X is the total number of documents of pertinent interest included in a given system.   See also Noise Factor, Pertinency Factor, Resolution Factor.

Resolution Factor.   The fraction of the total number of documents to which attention is directed in a search. $\frac{M}{N}$, where M is defined with the term noise factor and N is the total number of documents in a given system.   See also Noise Factor, Recall Factor, Pertinency Factor.

Retrieval.   See Information Retrieval.

Reverse Code Dictionary.   Alphabetic or numero alphabetic
    arrangement of codes, associated with their correspond-
    ing English words or terms.   See also Code Dictionary.

*Role Indicators.   Codes for synthetic relationships which are
    used to indicate how various entities, attributes, proc-
    esses, etc. were reported to have been involved in some
    experiment or observed phenomenon.

Routine (Computers).   A set of coded instructions arranged
    in proper sequence to direct the computer to perform a
    desired operation or series of operations.   See also
    Program (noun).

Screening.   The preliminary selection of documents or rec-
    ords containing information in order to faciliate subse-
    quent processing or identification of pertinent items.

Search Strategy.   A mathematical analysis and formulation
    of the various methods by which a certain literature
    search may be carried out and the determination of the
    most advantageous method of locating desired information.

Searching.   The activity involved in inspecting a single
    record, a file of such records, or any representation of
    contents in code or other form.   See also Selecting.

Self-demarcating Codes.   Codes in which the symbols are so
    arranged and selected that the generation of false combi-
    nations by interaction of segments from two successive
    codes is prevented.

Selecting.   The activity involved in merely identifying or in
    actually physically removing a record or records from
    a file (which see).   See also Searching.

*Semantic Factors.   Generic concepts used to indicate im-
    portant aspects of meaning of terms of more specific
    nature.   For instance, the specific term "thermometer"
    might be related to three semantic factors "temperature, "
    "measure, " and "device, "

Set.   A number of things having one or more characteristics
    in common.

--

Sorting. (1) The arranging of related documents, either alphabetically, numerically, or by class, done either manually or by machine. (2) The activity involved in arranging graphic records according to certain arbitrary criteria. These criteria may be selected and made explicit either prior to or at the time that the records are physically arranged. See also Searching and Seclecting.

Specific Characteristic. A characteristic (which see) which applies to a lesser number of graphic records or objects than a generic characteristic.

*Subject Classification. The technique of filing or arranging units of knowledge by means of symbolic forms under headings which denote the logical relationship of a number of such units.

Symbolic Logic. A system of logical rules and symbols to facilitate exact reasoning about non-numerical factual matter and relationships. A branch of the subject known as Boolean algebra has been of considerable assistance in the logical design of computing circuits. Also called "mathematical logic."

Synthetic Relationship. A relation existing between concepts which pertains to empirical observation. Such relationships are involved, not in defining concepts or terms, but in reporting the results of observations and experiments.

Telegraphic Abstracts. Stylized abstracts, in which the relationships between the various materials, processes, and products are made explicit through the use of Role Indicators (which see) and an elementary artificial syntax. recorded with the aid of Barriers (which see).

Terminal Digit Posting. The arrangement and recording of serial numbers of documents on the basis of the final digits of the numbers.

Theory of Games. The characterization of games of skill in terms of mathematical models, first proposed by von Neumann and Morgenstern.

Uniterm Cards. Cards on each of which an individual word indicates some subject aspect of documents, whose serial numbers are also listed. See Terminal Digit Posting.

Uniterming.   The selection of words, considered to be im-
    portant for later retrieval from articles, reports, or
    other documents which are to be included in a Uniterm
    index. Compare "Indexing, " "Word indexing".

Uniterm System.   An information retrieval system which uses
    Uniterm cards (which see). Cards representing words of
    interest in a search are selected and compared visually.
    If identical numbers are found to appear on the Uniterm
    card, undergoing comparison, these numbers represent
    documents to be examined in connection with the search.

UNIVAC.   One of a series of electronic digital computers
    produced by the Remington-Rand Division of Sperry-Rand
    Corp.

Universal Decimal Classification.   A classification system
    based on the Dewey Decimal Classification, but expanded
    with various symbols to show relationships between
    classes, time span, country involved, etc.

W.R.U. Searching Selector.   An experimental machine built
    to scan encoded abstracts recorded on punched paper tape,
    and to perform complex logical operations in the selection
    of pertinent documents.

Word Indexing.   Indexing based on the selection of words as
    used in document, without giving thought to synonyms and
    more generic concepts related to the term selected.

X-794.   An experimental IBM machine designed to scan en-
    coded abstracts recorded on punched cards and to perform
    complex logical operations in the selection of pertinent
    documents. See also W.R.U. Searching Selector.

Zatocoding.   A system of random, superimposed coding
    (which see) recorded by edge-notching cards, developed
    by C. N. Mooers.

SYMBOL INDEX

(The page number listed after a symbol is the first one on which the symbol is defined or discussed.)

INDEX

www.ingramcontent.com/pod-product-compliance
Lightning Source LLC
Chambersburg PA
CBHW071158050326
40689CB00011B/2157